Sky Painter

Sky Painter

The Story of Robert Newton Hurley

by

Jean Swanson

WESTERN PRODUCER BOOK SERVICE
SASKATOON
1973

WESTERN PRODUCER BOOK SERVICE
SASKATOON, SASKATCHEWAN

Printed and Bound in Canada by Modern Press
ISBN 0-919306-40-3

Sky Painter has been produced with the help of a Canada Council block grant, which has made possible the inclusion of more color plates than would have been possible without such assistance.

For the hundreds who own
Hurley paintings and treasure
them as something lovely

Hurley at his worktable, Victoria, 1971

R. H. Macdonald

Preface

SKY PAINTER is intended to be an informal biography of a popular artist, not a penetrating study of his work. As source material I have relied almost exclusively on memoirs Mr. Hurley wrote in 1966 of his life up to 1927, and on diaries he kept in 1938 and from 1950 to 1958, all of which are included in the Hurleyana Collection in the Shortt Library of Canadiana at the University of Saskatchewan, Saskatoon Campus, and on articles, clippings, and scores of personal letters which are preserved both in the Shortt Library and in his private collection. I have also used material in my own files relating to the history of art in Saskatoon, and books about the history of Saskatoon and the history of painting in Canada. I had many consultations with the artist, and with Mrs. Hurley, in the winter of 1972 in Victoria.

I thank the librarians at the Saskatoon Public Library and at the Murray Memorial Library at the University of Saskatchewan for their interest and for helping to make my research easy and pleasant: in particular, Mrs. Frances Morrison, chief librarian, Saskatoon Public Library; Wilbur Lepp, librarian in charge of the local history room at the Public Library; Mrs. P. W. McMeans, librarian at the J. S. Wood branch of the Public Library; D.C. Appelt, university librarian; and Mrs. A. L. La Brash, university reference librarian.

The paintings selected for reproduction were chosen for four reasons: First, to show the main types of his painting — the skies, the prairie landscapes, the abstracts, the aerial scenes, and the West Coast work; secondly, to indicate the extent of his sketching area; thirdly, to harmonize with the story of his life; and fourthly, to illustrate, in a general way, the change in his work from the 1930's to the 1960's, especially his gradual elimination of details.

I thank R. H. Macdonald, executive editor of *The Western Producer* and chairman of the Prairie Books Committee, and his editorial assistant, Jennifer Evans, for their diligent search through many collections for paintings which would match, in mood and spirit and subject, ones which Mr. Hurley and I had selected from his color slides as appropriate ones to accompany the story of his work and life. I am greatly indebted to Mr. Macdonald for having asked me to undertake the work.

Hundreds of names could have been included. I have kept them to a minimum, deliberately, in order not to overburden Mr. Hurley's life story with the names of his patrons and in order not to offend some patrons by mentioning others. I chose names which frequently crept into the story through his writings and his conversations, but to him all his patrons are precious. I also deliberately refrained from consulting his host of friends so that his story would not turn into a succession of anecdotes. To a great extent, *Sky Painter* is Robert Hurley's own story, even to the point of using many of his expressions to describe his experiences.

It should be mentioned that a great many persons named in this story are no longer living, but with one or two exceptions, reference to their death has not been made as it had no relevance to the role they played in Hurley's life.

Permission to quote from *Painting in Canada A History,* by J. Russell Harper, was granted by The University of Toronto Press, Toronto; from *September Gale: A Study of Arthur Lismer of the Group of Seven,* by John A. B. McLeish, by J. M. Dent & Sons (Canada) Ltd., Don Mills, Ontario; from *The Technique of Water-Colour Painting,* by Leonard Richmond and J. Littlejohns, by the Pitman Publishing Company, London, England; and from *I'll Take the Train,* by Ken Liddell, by Prairie Books, Saskatoon.

J. S.   April, 1973

Contents

INDEX OF ILLUSTRATIONS

INDEX OF COLOR PLATES

1

"Proud of Our Sky"

"MANY, MANY THANKS FOR THE Hurley which arrived yesterday. Until I saw the picture I couldn't know that it was exactly what I wanted. I could not be more delighted with it — and, I'm afraid, a bit too anxious to get more Hurleys. Claude Butler, who is our general manager and who lived in Prince Albert for about ten years, came into my office when I had it propped up on my desk yesterday and greeted me with 'What are you doing with Saskatchewan?' " (From a letter to the author, December, 1953, from Anne Park, traveling representative for Ambassador Books in Toronto.)

Over the last forty years the hundreds and hundreds who have purchased Hurley paintings have been motivated strongly by the power of the artist to depict a particular kind of landscape with which they have been familiar or impressed. He expressed the landscape as a symbol of his response to it, and in turn, his paintings became symbolic of Saskatchewan for the general public. The immediate and compelling impact of his subject matter over-shadowed serious recognition of his work as an artist. It is only recently that an interest in the artistry of his painting has exceeded a fascination with the subject, although isolated instances of critical appreciation have appeared since the early 1940's.

Hurley's name will not be found in any history of Canadian painting, nor are his paintings represented in the country's National Gallery in Ottawa. If those are measures of a painter's worth, then Hurley scores a zero. On the other hand, he has been signally recognized by Saskatchewan, his adopted province, and by the University of Saskatchewan at Saskatoon. In addition, his paintings have been presented to more visiting dignitaries and sought by more VIP's than the works of any other prairie artist.

In J. Russell Harper's *Painting in Canada A History* (University of Toronto Press, 1966) there is mention of only one other Canadian painter, Marc-Aurèle Fortin, in Quebec, who had a following similar to Robert Newton Hurley's and for somewhat the same reason. ". . . every cultured French-Canadian home around Montreal in the 1930s," writes Mr. Harper, "had a Fortin landscape: they were purchased partly because the subject-matter was so typical of the beloved Province of Quebec and was painted by one of its sons, and partly because it was the accepted thing to do." So with Mr. Hurley: it was the accepted and popular thing to have a Hurley painting, and with the proliferation of styles in the forties and fifties, it became comfortable to buy his work. The many who beat a path to his door had the assurance that they were in good company and they could come out quite boldly with the cliché, "I don't know a thing about art, but I know what I like."

And like Mr. Hurley's paintings they did, particularly the sky effects and the nocturnes (Plates II, III, XIV, XVI, XXIX, XXX). As Edward McCourt wrote: "We westerners are immensely proud of our sky and never tire of calling attention to its scope, clarity and delicate colour-shades." (*The Yukon and Northwest Territories*, The Macmillan Company of Canada Limited, Toronto, 1969.) If there were such a category of painting as a skyscape, Hurley would be one of its most peerless practitioners.

The Prairies affect people in many ways. Even those who find them monotonous, find the monotony overwhelming. In the days before air travel became usual and before diesel engines whisked their coaches across the land at record speeds; in the days, that is, of slow trains and many stops, it was customary to see travelers take up books or packs of cards to help to pass the time across the plains. Only those who had fallen under the spell of the Prairies would gaze raptly out of the windows; for the others it was a land with no "scenery."

Living on the Prairies could be a devastating experience for those accustomed to gentle and verdant surroundings. Mr. McCourt described what effects loneliness and fear could have on a young Irish immigrant in *Home is the Stranger* (Macmillans, Toronto, 1950). His Norah's rebellion against the bleak environment was usual enough to arouse a sympathetic response from many readers. Conversely, life on the Prairies could be a most exhilarating experience, as evidenced in many of the memoirs of pioneers, such as Mary Hiemstra's *Gully Farm* (McClelland & Stewart Limited, Toronto, 1955) where the Yorkshire parents conquered their initial homesickness and grew to love "The Land of Promise Fulfilled."

Whatever one's reaction to traveling across or living on the Prairies may be, the sky, as the star of the drama, always captures attention and often arouses admiration and awe. Come sunset time, most travelers will stare out of the windows of trains or roadside diners, and most dwellers will cease from whatever they are doing to watch for a few minutes the invariably splendid show, sometimes of a brilliance inconceivable to those who have not been eyewitnesses. And when the moon shines on snow-covered fields and on the roofs of the looming black shapes of elevators with such a brightness that one can almost read by its light, the magic is of the arresting kind, worth a walk or a drive even in forty-below temperatures.

It was not the frightening or desolate aspect of the Prairies that Hurley loved to paint so much as their wonder and beauty and, often, their fruitfulness (Plate IV). If, in his paintings, he didn't make a great statement about life, at least he made a near-perfect one within the limitations he himself set, and it was a statement that attracted hundreds of admirers.

Ironically, Hurley's admirers dictated the course his career as an artist would follow, for to paint what appealed to the many often took on the nature of a chore for the artist. There were times when he felt that the quality of his paintings was mediocre, as when, at the beginning of 1954, he reviewed his work over the past year and concluded that he had done nothing "new or exciting." He was to repeat the complaint often as the demands for his "skies" prevented him from working on his abstracts.

In this respect, too, his career ran parallel to Fortin's, for Fortin was "never appreciated in the way he would have liked." But there the resemblance ends, for Fortin had a "turbulent" soul and refused to paint always to please his public. Hurley, like Fortin, was a restless individual, but he had nothing of the rebel in him. If the public wanted nocturnes and sunsets, the public would have them; he had to steal time to spend on the creation of other kinds of painting. Hurley would have liked to have gained recognition for his abstracts, but his followers, on the whole, chose otherwise. The type of work which really fascinated him is shown in Plates V, VI, XVII, XVIII, XIX and XX. "The Crystals" was based on a twenty-sided figure that attracted his attention in the laboratory of Dr. H. H. Ferns, then head of the mathematics department at the University of Saskatchewan, and it shows his delight in shaping colors. In "Shorebirds" and "Herons" he outlined birds with the least possible number of lines for the design, and achieved a decorative effect of delicate beauty. But the consensus was that his abstracts — particularly of birds and fish — were too stylized. Certainly, his abstracts were never conceived in the epic manner of Fortin's escapes from the Quebec landscape, such as his "Fighting Bulls," in which the sheer strength of the adversaries is emphasized (in the P. Bronfman collection in Montreal and reproduced in *Painting in Canada*). Hurley's, with their decorative delicacy, are reminiscent of the subtlety of Oriental art.

Yet, in another respect, their paintings have a touch in common. Mr. Harper writes of Fortin that "he was never nationalistic in his feelings, and was too complex to be seduced by any picture-making formula such as a reliance on rhythmical line or rigid stylization. . . . a religious overtone often lifts Fortin's work above the danger of mere illustrations." Hurley was more childlike than complex, but his religious fervor, which touched everything he created, saved even his most apparent "potboilers" from being insincere, and his most stylized abstracts from being only decorative.

In the confines of nine by twelve inches, or ten by fourteen, which were the measurements for most of Hurley's paintings, he could not be particularly daring. He could, however, achieve exquisite results. If his prolixity reflected a facility born of constant practice, it seldom reflected any sloppiness. He was too conscientious an artist and too decent an individual to pass off exercises on people he respected — his public.

Following closely on the letter quoted at the start of this chapter came another from a publisher's representative in Toronto: "Anne showed me the water color that you found for her and I admired it immensely. It really is a beautiful piece of work and if the artist (Mr. Hurley, I believe) would care to sell one of his pictures to me I'd certainly be delighted. If you can arrange this for me I shall be most grateful to you . . . Anne mentioned what she paid for hers to me, and that same amount or $5.00 or $10.00 more would not matter." (Letter from Evelyn Weatherill of British Book Service Limited, Toronto, January, 1954.)

She was another Easterner who wanted some of Saskatchewan. On her next trip West she called on Mr. Hurley and selected two of his paintings, a sunset and a fish abstract. What is interesting about her letter is her reference to the prices. Mr. Hurley rarely charged as much as twenty-five dollars for a water color, and usually he was content with fifteen or twenty. The smaller ones were available at five or ten dollars, depending on the affluence of the purchaser.

So, in addition to the sure-fire appeal of the subject matter, Hurley paintings were within the reach of everyman from the point of view of money. The appeal-price combination was so alluring that he sold his paintings by the hundreds, nearly exhausting himself in the process.

Mr. Hurley became a sort of prairie phenomenon, like Bible Bill Aberhart, the man who brought Social Credit to its triumph in Alberta, and Eye Opener Bob Edwards, the journalist who could make strong men tremble if they stepped out of line. The wide-open Canadian West is a land which encourages individualism and gives the nod to nonconformity. Where did Mr. Hurley come from? Who and what was he? In some respects his story is drab and dreary; in others, it's fantastic!

The Early Hurley

THE RELATIONSHIP between the first thirty-five years of Hurley's life and the rest of it has nothing of any obvious significance except in a negative way. In his own opinion there is such a complete separation between the two phases of his life that he could be regarded as the exception to prove the truth of the old saying that the tree will grow as the twig is bent.

Negatively, the relationship might prove to be a goldmine for a probing psychologist. Did the boy from the slums, did the young man who drifted aimlessly from job to job, feel the cold shoulder of respectability and affluence to a point where he later became somewhat overproud of recognition from solid citizens and distinguished visitors? Did the boy who received only a grade six education become too sensitive about his lack of education when he became a successful artist? Was not the boy whose father was a renegade Catholic, and was not the young man who saw no purpose or guiding principle in life, who walked with loneliness and despair, was he not ripe for conversion when exposed to evangelistic fervor? A psychiatrist would not be hard pressed to find the boy in the man; but for Hurley, the suggestions would be purely academic, and his answers to any questions attempting to connect his earlier life with his later would simply deny a connection of any kind.

He came to believe that a Divine Power had kept him from harm and had directed his steps to Canada, but he holds only himself responsible for his mistakes and failures before he recognized that Power.

Charles and Hannah Hurley had a large family. Of the nine children who survived beyond infancy, Robert Newton, named after an uncle, was the youngest. When he was born, March the twenty-sixth, 1894, the Hurleys lived at Number 16, Perring Street, Devon's Road, Bromley-by-Bow, London. It was a small but self-contained house in the midst of row-housing on a deadend street in a slum district where the gangs were rough, the rats fat and fierce, and the stench terrible. The windows were fitted with wooden shutters which were bolted on the inside at night as protection against neighborhood toughs; Charles, the oldest son, carried a stout club to and from his work at Spratt's biscuit factory to ward off rats. The yard was a concrete area, with no soil for even a lone plant. It measured about fifteen by twenty feet, and was surrounded by a brick wall ten feet high. In it were the water closet, and the cages or cotes where brother Charlie kept his pigeons. Between the parish of Bow and nearby West Ham, in the 1890's, there was a lot of open, marshy land occupied by hundreds of birds which the gypsies caught and sold, so "Young Bob," as the family called him, was not entirely a concrete-jungle denizen.

Inside Number 16, there was heartiness and warmth and worry. The father, Charles Randall Hurley, was an easy-going man, half-Irish, who loved the pleasures of the world beyond all else, his three passions being his lively wife, his clay pipe, and the local pub, which functioned under the equivocal sign "The Good Intent." Across from The Good Intent was a gospel church called Devon's Road Lighthouse, ever ready to come to the aid of those whose good intentions led them towards the inevitable place. Unfortunately for the Hurley family, the Lighthouse had no appeal for Father Charles, whose taste for alcohol eventually meant serious deprivations for the children.

Young Bob was particularly fond of the Christmas season, which began with the making of the plum pudding. There was a fruit-preparation session with everyone helping, and when the ingredients were mixed, Father contributed a bottle of Irish whisky. All the helpers took three stirs before the heady mixture was poured into bags to be boiled in a vast copper kettle. It was during one of the pudding times that Bob was given the only spanking he ever received from his father. The boy reached out to help himself to an irresistible bit of fruit. His sister Nellie slapped his hand, and hurt and disappointed, he reacted by throwing his chopping knife at her, cutting her arm. Father settled the dispute. The ruffled feelings calmed down as final preparations for the festivities occupied all their attention. The father, as usual, looked after the ordering and roasting of a boar's head and a twenty-pound joint of beef for Christmas dinner, while the mother and girls prepared a great ham which they served with red cabbage and onion pickles for a Christmas midnight snack. It became a family Christmas-day tradition for the father to sing favorite songs and to do his version of "The Irish Immigrant." The mother sang "While Shepherds Watched." Carolers, of whatever denomination, were always invited in for tea and mince pies.

Singing came as naturally to the Hurleys as to the birds. They all sang. The most famous singer of the family was Uncle Alfred Hurley who was known in the London of the nineties as The Irish Tenor. With a Mr. Crowder he operated The Parthenon, a popular music hall which still exists as a motion picture house. Singing has continued to be one of Bob's delights, and in middle age, as he became more and more familiar with classical masterpieces, he acquired the pastime of adapting airs from them for his favorite hymns.

Uncle Alfred was a clerk in the Bank of England, but his appearance at a music hall was not a particularly novel venture for the son of a man who had operated a similar kind of British institution — a pub. Charles Randall Hurley, Bob's grandfather, had come to England in the middle of the nineteenth century from Dunmanway, County Cork, Ireland, where the Hurley name was variously spelled — "O'Hurley," "O'Herlithy," "O'Hiely." Hundreds of other Irish left their land at the same time, and many of them settled in the London slum district of Bethnal Green and found employment as dock workers. Hurley's grandfather set up a pub, which flourished well enough that he was able to provide his three children — Alfred, Elizabeth, and Charles — with a good education in the Roman Catholic parochial school. Hurley's grandmother, however, was not a Catholic, but a descendant of a Huguenot family who had fled from France after the St. Bartholomew's Massacre (1572). The mixture of religions and racial backgrounds diluted any strong convictions, and the dilution continued when Robert's father married a Protestant girl, Hannah Mills.

Handsome Charles Hurley, red-headed and red-bearded, had been a member of the Metropolitan Police when he met and fell in love with Hannah. The wearing of a beard was a condition of employment with the London police in the 1870's. Hannah didn't like the carroty beard. Charles left the police force. Having some skill as a blacksmith and a worker in copper, he obtained a job as chief saw filer at Silverton's Limited, a company that owned cable-laying, ocean-going ships. Hannah settled down to care for her smooth-shaven husband and their many children — Elizabeth (Lizzie), Charles, Margaret, Alice, Ellen (Nellie), Arthur, Hannah, Miriam, and Robert Newton.

When Bob was born, the older members of the family were either away from home in domestic service or out all day at their jobs. Their father, unlike his father, was unable to provide his children with an education beyond the elementary level. He had a steady job; he also had a steady appetite for alcohol.

Nellie or Arthur, who were still at home, would sometimes take Bob to visit their oldest sister Lizzie, in service as a cook at Major Brown's establishment near Regent's Park — Major Brown wrote a column about racing under the pseudonym "Pegasus" for a London paper, and Lizzie worked for him until she retired. After a meal with Lizzie, they would tarry awhile at the nearby zoo, where Bob liked the tropical bird section best; but the ritual of feeding the lions was not to be missed.

When Bob was seven the family moved to 28 Oakfield Road in the outer London area of East Ham in Essex so his father could have a handier bus route to Silverton's. He left behind his childhood chum, Harry Fiveash, stepson of Mr. Horlock, the landlord of all the houses on Perring Street.

The Horlocks lived in a house that boasted a large garden where there was a greenhouse and an aquarium to fascinate the children, and where chickens, ducks, rabbits, goats, and kids ran around them as they played. There was an added fascination about the establishment — Mrs. Horlock, before she was married, had worked for *Royalty,* which was as thrilling to Bob as having been close enough to the Queen to be able to reach out and touch her.

The house on Oakfield Road had a little garden, much to the mother's delight, and a big sycamore tree, which has remained silhouetted in Hurley's memory. Beyond East Ham were wide fertile fields of market gardens, an inviting walk region. Often, on a Sunday, Bob's father would take him for a walk through the gardens and would stop in at The Good Intent before going home, leaving the boy to spend a long hour or so staring at the large pictures of hunting scenes in India that filled the windows; or perhaps it would be in front of The Widow's Son's Arms, where he would wonder about the widow's son who had left home on a Good Friday years before and had never returned, a circumstance that started the tradition, still carried on, of topping the tavern's sign with a hot cross bun every Good Friday.

To the south of East Ham were the Royal Albert docks, and for many years another favorite excursion was to the docks to watch the sailing vessels. Arthur, who later worked as a packing case maker at Silverton's, made models of the ships and also spent hours making water-color sketches of activities on the Thames. Bob watched and admired his brother, but felt no urge to take up a brush.

During World War I, when their children had all left home, Charles and Hannah Hurley moved from Oakfield Road to smaller quarters in London. The family home was taken over by their daughter Margaret and her husband Abe Matthews, a railway ticket collector in East Ham. Two of their children, Len, a magistrate in East Ham, and Lillian, a missionary worker, still live at Number 28.

Bob had started his education at the usual age of five at St. Paul's Road School. At East Ham he and his sister Miriam went off to Plasket Land Council School, where he finished his primary and only education. He left school at the end of grade six when he was fourteen, in 1908. His preferred subjects had been geography and literature, but he hadn't shown decided promise along any particular line. His interest in geography probably was the root of his fondness for travel books in later years; and his ability at grammar and composition laid the foundation for his writing attempts throughout his life. He always liked words as words, and one of his favorite amusements in later life became the composing of tongue-twisters and nonsense rhymes.

In the fall of 1972, for instance, while regaining his strength after an operation, he amused himself by composing limericks and sent a sample one in a letter:

> *An Arab shiek of Morocco*
> *Was drinking a cup of hot cocoa (kokko)*
> *A spider fell in,*
> *He swapped it for gin,*
> *Which made him a wee bit "rocco."*

He likes the music in many operas but isn't entranced by the "screeching" in foreign tongues. In a postscript to a letter written on his seventy-eighth birthday (March 26, 1972, Sunday) he remarked that he tuned in the day before to a brilliant performance by the Metropolitan Opera of Donizetti's "Daughter of the Regiment." As an opera by any other name would sound as sweet in a foreign language, he playfully suggested that it might have been called "Son of a Gun" by Macaronio Spagetti.

At one time, when the Beatles were at the height of their popularity and had been honored by the Queen — 1965 — he considered publishing a small volume of his verses, with illustrations by the author, for, he wrote, "if those awful distortions of the melodic line, and disgusting contortions, and manufacturers of cacophony can get away with it, so should I with these 'noble' lyrics."

No one teacher influenced Bob in any way, but one master who was in charge of entertainments and who organized a minstrel show made use of a homemade percussion instrument the operation of which Hurley has brought to an unbelievable degree of perfection over the years. The instrument is within the means of anyone who knows a butcher, but the playing of it requires more manual skill than the use of chopsticks, and a highly developed sense of rhythm. The instrument is, simply, two beef rib bones, boiled, dried, and polished. With them, Mr. Hurley can accompany music by almost any composer (though perhaps not the Beatles), and he can produce a wide variety of sounds, from clacks to purrs. The set he possesses now is quite old, having been obtained from Mont E. Rayner, a Saskatoon merchant perhaps best known as being the father of Chuck Rayner, a one-time star hockey player for the New York Rangers. The bones are about eight inches long and so hard they could be mistaken for relics from the Stone Age.

Bob kicked cans around the streets and the schoolyard and played the usual rough-and-tumble games with his classmates. He didn't even think about sports. The Hurleys were too poor. He lived near the West Ham football grounds and the game became the one spectator sport that he enjoyed, particularly since brother Charlie played for the team of his pub, The British Empire. At home, being short of paper, Bob amused himself doing scribbles of football teams in action on the blank pages of *Pilgrim's Progress, Huckleberry Finn, Ben Hur,* and the novels of Rider Haggard and Charles Dickens — one of his sisters belonged to a Dickensian club. His scribbles weren't pictures; they were just the sort of doodling in which most people indulge from time to time.

Jaunts to the Tower Bridge were a highlight of his schoolboy days. The boys would wait until the bridge was adjusted for the passage of a tall ship when the center part was lifted, forming a high level walk reached by steps. They would rush up the stairs and walk along the upper level, enjoying the view of London and no doubt spitting or dropping pebbles into the water far below. And London Tower drew them like a magnet with its evidences of gory history and its collection of glittering jewels. Bob was a poor kid from an unhappy home — because of his father's drinking habit — but he didn't become involved with a tough gang, perhaps because of the affectionate care of his mother, sisters, and brothers.

Even if he had been bright at school, as was his sister Alice, he would not have been able to have continued. After the age of fourteen, it cost money to go to school. Bob went to work. Between 1908 and 1923 when he emigrated to Canada, not counting the three years from 1917 to 1920 that he spent in the army, he had about fifteen jobs. And he was always stony broke.

The jobs he had were so dreary and so poorly paid that there was no incentive to continue at them. For instance, he distributed samples of polish to housewives from the Brasso Company and was paid a shilling a day; he washed bottles for a ginger beer factory; he fitted the ribs into umbrellas for a manufacturing concern; he was an assistant bartender in a pub that catered to dock laborers; he was a dockie at the Royal Albert docks where cargoes that contained tempting items like Nestlé's sweet chocolate and ladies' silk stockings and undergarments were rifled by the stevedores and sold in the coffee shops and pubs; he was a sorter in a seed house.

In between the London jobs, he took employment on the land, partly because he wanted to see some of the country and partly because he was of a restless disposition — a rolling stone. The first land work he did was in 1910 when he went to Devonshire in the care of a group of people known as the "London Lads — County Work Society," sponsored by the Anglican Church. He worked for a Mr. Northmore in a deep valley by a trout stream known as the Meavy on a farm called Lower Goodameavy. His wages were about five shillings a month, and to earn them he cut ferns for bedding for the herds of Dartmoor ponies that were corralled into the yard each year. Once when he was in the hedges he was arrested by two guards looking for a convict escaped from Dartmoor prison.

From Lower Goodameavy he went to a farm near Land's End and learned to clean and set up a cream separator, pick and grade apples, and cut brush. He stayed there for six months, then back to London and one of the many jobs, then back to a farm in Yorkshire where his work was tending the dairy herd and taking the herd bull to the pool for a drink. One day the bull charged at him, and it was with this occasion in mind that he commented years later that he was sure a Guiding Power had kept him from disaster.

Hurley was in London when World War I began. He tried to enlist but was rejected because of his eyesight. Despondent and restless again, he called on his sister Lizzie in Regent's Park, had dinner with her, then went off with his pack and a few shillings on a walking trip to Wales, sleeping in the roadside ditches by night.

There was work on a farm in Shropshire for a few months, then he found his way to his sister Nell, who had married Tom Copley, a foreman iron molder at Crittal's Foundry, Braintree, Essex. Bob found some work helping with one of the dairy herds in the district. In the evenings they often went to the pub where Tom was always made welcome with free beer while he played the piano, a good bargain for those who offered the beer, for Tom preferred playing to drinking.

Late in 1915 an opportunity came for Bob to join an auxiliary branch of the army and go to France to relieve workers there for duty at the front lines. He crossed over to Boulogne-sur-Mer, where he stayed three months, unloading ammunition and working in a cafe for soldiers, before the urge for something new came over him again. He was under no obligation to remain, so back to England he went, enduring the experience of seasickness on the way.

Between 1908 and 1917, there was a period of two years — around 1908 to 1910 — when he applied himself to learning a trade which he and his family thought would likely be his life's work. He was accepted as an apprentice by Terry & Company, Printers of Hatton Garden, and was to be trained to be a compositor. The printing shop was located in Shoe Lane, just off Fleet Street, and was run by Gibson and Sons. His hours were from eight in the morning until six. On Saturdays they quit at noon, but Bob, being the young lad in the shop, had to remain to clean all the presses.

In addition to learning to set type, his duties included going after tea or beer for the men every morning and afternoon. He carried a long pole, in which were set the mugs with the men's names on them. At the end of the week, each man gave him a penny for his troubles. Bob disliked the printing shop and the roughness of the men there, and he found the work a strain on his eyes. An eye examination revealed that he had seriously impaired vision, so while he had served only two years of his seven-year apprenticeship, he was released. It was the one and only time he was grateful for his poor eyes.

However, the two years in the printing plant were the most important years of his working life in England, not because of what he learned in the shop but because of what he picked up on his way to and from work. He rode the underground from Upton Park to Mark Lane and then he walked the two miles to Shoe Lane, past St. Paul's and down Fleet Street. The sights and sounds and smells of the great city were indelibly impressed on him. The National Gallery and the British Museum were along the route he could follow, and if anything in the early years made an impression on the boy who was to become the water-color interpreter of the Canadian plains, it was the water colors of J. M. W. Turner and of John Sell Cotman in those two institutions.

He was immediately attracted by the Turner section in the National Gallery, and when he discovered that there were hundreds of Turner "gems of light" under cover in the basement to protect them from fading, he spent hours going through them and enjoying them as an escape from the drabness of his existence.

In the British Museum, where one can spend a lifetime and still have more to see and to learn, he singled out the water colors of Cotman as his special delight. They mesmerized him, and became photographed in his mind for all time. What appealed to him most was their beautiful simplicity, the elimination of inessentials, a quality which was to be a characteristic of his own work. It was the sheer purity of their simplicity that held him spellbound. "Simple," "simplicity," are words that have been often applied to Hurley's life and work, but never in the sense of artlessness or homeliness; always in the sense of purity, clarity, unification.

Almost from the beginning of his painting career, Robert Hurley has followed the practice of making quick pencil sketches of scenes that have caught his imagination, and writing in their color patterns; or, if without paper and pencil handy, he kept the scenes in his memory until he had an opportunity to jot them down. It is not surprising, therefore, that the paintings he imprinted on his memory at a very impressionable time of his life should have played their part in directing his talents along similar lines. To this extent, he was influenced by the Cotman water colors, and to a lesser degree by the Turners.

The hours that he spent traveling between Mark Lane and Shoe Lane while he worked at his uncongenial trade were not time wasted. And it is certainly not hindsight to catch a glimpse of a future artist in an unschooled teenager who spent hours of his little enough spare time gazing at water colors. One wonders how many boys of his age and class would have so occupied themselves!

In 1917, the Kaiser's war, as Bob's generation called it, was going so badly for the Allies that men who had been rejected previously were being accepted into the armed services. After a medical at Whitehall, Bob became Private Robert Newton Hurley, No. 665181, attached to the 1st Garrison Battalion of the 1st Suffolk Regiment, and he was sent off for his basic training to the Isle of Grain, County Kent. Before his unit was ready for duty the war had taken a turn for the better, and it was the farms not the front lines that were desperately in need of help. On his way to a farm in Shropshire, he had a long wait at a London depot and used the time to make a quick call on his family. He missed the train and spent a week in jail for being AWOL.

From jail he went to Yockleton, near Wales, where Mr. Jones, the farmer, had a large steam thresher and did custom work for the neighbors and for the Shewsbury asylum. Those inmates who were considered of the harmless variety were allowed to help with the farm work, but Robert, whose task involved the use of a sharp knife to cut twine, played it safe and asked to be relieved of their enthusiastic assistance. When they were finished the asylum work and he was waiting for the boss's son Tom to settle the accounts, he struck up a conversation with a fellow who was standing around and happened to mention that before he had joined the army he had worked at the Royal Albert docks. "I know that district well," said the man. "I built the Towbury docks." Being in jail had not been pleasant, but he had at least had a better sense of safety there than when working near the asylum.

In the vicinity of Yockleton was a cone-shaped hill called Wreken. On a day off, Bob walked to it, climbed to the top, and looked across the miles to Mount Snowdon and the hills of North Wales. It was his first "aerial" view; it delighted him then as aerial views were to do forty years later.

It was at Yockleton that he painted his first water color, a small picture of the stone cow barn. The people at the farm liked it, so he presented it to Mr. Jones.

Hurley was detained after the Armistice at a large demobilization camp at Whitchurch, Shropshire, and was to proceed to France for guard duty when he received word of his father's death. He was granted compassionate leave to go to London for the funeral. His battalion had left when he returned to Whitchurch, so he was made a hut orderly, in charge of drawing rations. In 1920, he was given his official discharge and three pounds sterling.

Bob, at the age of twenty-six, had no more idea of what he wanted to do or what he wished to become than Young Bob had had at the age of fourteen, perhaps less, for Young Bob had had a couple of dreams about how he might make his fortune. Young Bob had heard, for instance, that there was good money to be made in writing songs. So he had written a song, which he had thought was pretty melodic, especially when sung by his brother Charlie, who was in great demand as a local entertainer — he had a voice, Hurley recalls, resembling Tennessee Ernie Ford's. But the song had been rejected. He also had had an idea that he could make money creating designs for commercial firms. He had done a design for a tea company. The company had rejected it. His dreams had died there and then. Perhaps he had been too easily discouraged, but as he had been daily aware of the need to earn his keep, he had been forced to find work with pay. It's one of the twists of his life story that when he needed money as a boy he had to give up any dreams of creative work, and when he didn't need money as an artist, he sacrificed what he considered his creative work to paint for the public.

In 1920 he boarded with his sister Margaret at the old family home and found a job excavating sand and gravel. He was depressed by the ugly cinderbrick homes that marred the lovely Essex countryside with its giant elm groves and big oaks. The years from 1920 to 1923 became a nightmare kind of time for him. One dreary day dragged into another dreary day. He could see no point in anything.

In 1923, while visiting his sister Alice at a seaside place in Kent, he made his first real sketch, a pencil drawing of a teapot and some kitchen utensils, and he discovered that the problems of perspective held no mystery for him. Perspective, he later wrote, came as naturally to him as breathing. Alice's husband, Harry Bull, who had worked in a munitions plant during the war and who now looked after some tennis courts, had heard that a Canadian Pacific Railway committee in London was selecting men for farm work in Canada and suggested that Bob might investigate.

Hurley went to the C.P.R. offices in Trafalgar Square. The fare, he learned, was twelve pounds. He didn't have twelve shillings. However, one of the officials noticed his service stripes and advised him to apply at another office a short distance away where servicemen were being screened. Because of his background of farm work, his application was successful. On his return to the C.P.R. office less than an hour later, he was given a free ticket to Canada on the *Empress of France.* He didn't know it then, but the money to help ex-servicemen emigrate to Canada had been put up by Lord Beaverbrook.

On August the fourth, 1923, "Young Bob" waved good-by to Nellie, Alice, and Lizzie at a London bus depot. The sisters had scraped together one pound, which he wore sewn in a belt under his clothes. It was the last he saw of any of his family.

He had little to show for his first thirty years of life. The singing Hurleys had left an impression. Whatever became of him, it was likely that he would continue singing and playing his harmonica as pleasant pastimes. His football doodles in the family's books, his brief experiment with commercial designs, his one water color, his few pencil drawings, added up to less than the "art" work done by most school children. The Turners and the Cotmans had given him pleasure, not inspiration. Nothing he had done presaged the future Hurley.

Sask. Photo Services

No wonder elevators became a sort of trade-mark of Hurley paintings. He had no lack of models, although not all towns boasted the number that are to be seen at Meadow Lake.

3

O God — O Canada! O God!

THE VOYAGE TO CANADA on the *Empress of France* was uneventful, except for one day of seasickness, and made no impression on Hurley, whose emotions were focused on his adventure. In Quebec, he took off his money belt and spent his precious pound on bread, biscuits, oranges, cheese, and cigarettes to take with him on the trip to Winnipeg, the end of the line for imported workers. Time passed quickly on the long journey, which at that time took four nights and three days, for there were more than 200 men on the train, all intent on games and pranks and get-togethers to pass the hours. It was the usual harvester excursion-type of transportation, not the height of luxury but acceptable to men who thought they were well off if they had some change to jingle in their pockets; few of them were of the tenderfoot breed. To Bob Hurley, who had been a transient worker up to then and knew what it was like to sleep under the sky or even on the wooden planks in a jail cell, the hard, slatted seats, the smoky stove, the all-pervasive smell of orange peel, coffee, beans, tomato soup, and whatever else the men found to heat, the grime, and the racket went largely unnoticed. There was singing, after a fashion, and he had his harmonica.

At Winnipeg Bob discovered that no harvesting employment had been arranged for the ex-servicemen whose fares had been paid to that point, so he applied to the C.P.R. office as a worker on a steel gang and was sent on to Milden, Saskatchewan, where new tracks were being laid across the farm lands, a spur line to serve the rich farming district.

At convenient points along the branch lines, which crisscrossed the prairie land like the marks left by skaters on a slough, grain elevators were erected to receive the bounty of the land before it was shipped across the country and across the world. The elevators became so characteristic a feature of the landscape that the fact that they were not indigenous to it became lost in their very familiarity. Old Indians and early settlers would remember the illimitable unmarked plains. Once the elevators and telephone lines were constructed, they became as much a part of the scene as the ground-hugging crocus in spring, the courageous little poplar groves, and the immensity of the sky, so often just a tremendous wash of beautiful blues and equally often the canvas for dramatic and ever-changing patterns of clouds, fabulous sunsets and dawns, brilliant sundogs, and the mysterious northern lights.

The elevators caught Hurley's eye as he traveled west from Winnipeg, and the ones at Milden soon became a landmark by which he judged direction and distance. Later, he remarked that he was impressed by the immense vistas and by the unique quality of the elevators. He was not, however, stirred esthetically by his surroundings, for he experienced that feeling of monotony and desolation which has disturbed or bored many newcomers to the Prairies.

At the time that Hurley was laying spikes on the ties in Saskatchewan, a bitter argument was going on in Eastern Canada about the selection of Canadian paintings for the British Empire Exhibition at Wembley in England.*

The traditionalists, led by the over-riding Sir Hector Charlesworth, of Toronto's *Saturday Night,* and S. Morgan-Powell, of the *Montreal Star,* two powerful dictators of Canadian taste, were exceedingly caustic in their comments about the favoritism shown to the works of the members of the Group of Seven by Eric Brown, the quiet, knowledgeable, and valiant head of the National Gallery in Ottawa. The Group of Seven men could be as bitingly articulate as their critics, and two of them, Arthur Lismer and A. Y. Jackson, were particularly vociferous in their defense of the new art.

The controversy over the work of the Group of Seven had raged for years. In the 1916 exhibition of the Ontario Society of Artists, for instance, J. E. H. MacDonald's "Tangled Garden" caused an uproar. It was likened by one critic to "the inside of a drunkard's stomach," a phrase which summed up the general attitude. After the fuss over the choice of paintings for the Wembley exhibition had died down, the academicians and the critics continued to damn the National Gallery for its practice of buying and exhibiting Group of Seven paintings. In 1925, Charlesworth referred to the Group's exhibition as a "chamber of horrors; a vision of things hard, glaring; repellent." That same year, A. Y. Jackson engaged in a public debate with E. Wyly Grier, a traditionalist but not a hidebound one. It became an episode of celebrated proportions — the report of it took five columns in the *Toronto Star;* its main value was that it aroused public interest. It was this debate that provided the *Star* with the quotable caption "IF COW CAN STAY IN PARLOR, THEN WHY CAN'T BULL MOOSE?" Jackson had been castigating the wealthy Canadian collectors for their philistinism, a favorite topic of his. "It was boasted in Montreal," he said, "that more Dutch art was sold there than in any other city on this continent. Dutch pictures became a symbol

*Details about the controversy over the work of the Group of Seven and also about Arthur Lismer's experiences in Western Canada and his opinions about art are derived from *September Gale: A Study of Arthur Lismer of the Group of Seven,* by John A. B. McLeish; J. M. Dent & Sons (Canada) Ltd., Toronto, 1955.

of social position and wealth. It was also whispered that they were a sound investment. . . . The houses bulged with cows, old women peeling potatoes, and windmills." He went on to describe what he and other Canadian artists like him were expressing: "Our atmosphere was clear and sharp, our colors were bright (crude if you will). . . . In summer it was green, raw greens all in a tangle; in autumn it flamed with red and gold; in winter it was wrapped in a blanket of dazzling snow, and in the springtime it roared with running waters and surged with new life — and yet our artists were advised to go to Europe and paint smelly canals! If a cow could stay in the drawing-room, then why couldn't a bull moose?"

Arthur Lismer also took an active part in the great controversy, always emphasizing the character of the country and the artist's responsibility to portray that character.

The continuing debate in Eastern Canada eventually produced national repercussions which had considerable impact on the development of art on the Prairies and so, indirectly, on the career of Robert Newton Hurley, for Hurley's success, in terms of recognition, was as much attributable to a favorable cultural environment as to his talent. The fight which Eric Brown, supported by Sir Edmund Walker, chairman of the National Gallery Board, and the Group of Seven waged for the recognition of Canadian art and the freedom of Canadian artists to express their environment in their own terms, was far reaching and long lasting. While Hurley was busy harrowing the farmers' fields, those few enlightened individuals were busy plowing the cultural ground so that better and richer produce would result. It was in the ground they plowed that Hurley flourished.

Hurley, the English adventurer, the immigrant laborer, had his way to make in the New World, and art certainly had no part in his plans. He had one concern — to make some money. Vaguely, in a deep recess of his mind, lay the idea that each experience might provide, sometime in the hazy future, source material for a writing career. The idea was never strong enough to prompt him to keep a notebook; nevertheless his photographic memory noted and retained details which men with purely materialistic aims would consider beside the point.

The job with the steel gang rather amused Bob, for the outfit had something of the quality of a circus. He recalled it, years later:

"Some specialists laid the ties, using a gauge to obtain correct alignment, then a derrick would swing the rails into place which in turn were spiked to the wooden ties. First came the derrick, then the tie car, then the steel rail flatcar, with the flatcar loaded with barrels of spikes next in line, then the tool and general supply car, and Foreman's and Timekeeper's office, and last but not least the all-important cook's kitchen, dining cars and sleeping cars, all resting on the last half mile of newly laid track. My first job was to lay spikes on the ties. A man on each side of the train doing the same operation, a sort of perpetual motion, as the whole circus would move at a snail's pace. At the day's close we could earn overtime by spiking down securely with sledge hammers those hastily laid iron spikes."

The track was being laid right through the middle of wheat fields. It was a bumper crop year, and the farmers lured the laborers away from the railway to work in the fields. Labor gaps were left in the steel gang, and Bob and his friend and working partner, Eddie Dawe, were shifted to the tie car. Eddie had also traveled on the *Empress of France,* but the two hadn't met until they reached Milden. Armed with a pickaroon — a sort of one-spike pickax — their job was to grab a heavy wooden tie and guide it onto a traveling conveyance which took it up front to the laying operation. It was hard labor, requiring the balance and agility of an acrobat, and after a few days Bob and Eddie called at the timekeeper's office for their final pay check. They were paid forty cents an hour, for a ten-hour day, with one dollar deducted for food and lodging.

The pair found harvest work with the Fish brothers of Plato, each receiving six dollars a day plus room and board. It was a large-scale operation which at harvest time centered around the running of a straw-burning threshing machine. The monster took seven bundle, or sheaf, wagons to keep it going. Threshing started after a five o'clock breakfast and continued into the night by the illumination of burning strawpiles. Bob was one of the wagon drivers,

Bob on a bundle wagon, Plato, Saskatchewan, 1923

the wagon being pulled by a team of Missouri mules. The two friends worked for ten days, then yielding to the hankering for city life, they collected their pay and headed for Saskatoon.

The men stayed at the YMCA on 20th Street and Spadina Crescent, a few short blocks to the theaters, cafes, and stores on Second Avenue, the main drag. Saskatoon was a city of about 25,000 in 1923, a friendly, bustling prairie center, proud of its reputation for Western hospitality and still boasting of its "Saskatoon Spirit."

The city's one high school, Nutana Collegiate Institute, had embarked in 1919 on its collection of paintings to commemorate students who had died in World War I. Dr. A. J. Pike and A. W. Cameron, of the collegiate staff, were the two moving spirits behind the memorial gallery, and the paintings they selected were those of the Group of Seven. At a time when the Group was fighting the traditionalists in the East, recognition and acceptance in the West were in the nature of the startling, for in Ontario, Saskatchewan was considered almost beyond the fringe of civilization. Yet about half of the members of the faculty of the fifteen-year-old University of Saskatchewan had come from Eastern Canada by way of such world-famous institutions of learning as Columbia, Yale, Harvard, the University of Chicago, Oxford, Cambridge, and the Sorbonne in Paris; the other half had come from England, Ireland, Scotland, France, Germany, and the United States of America.

The University of Saskatchewan was no prairie Heidelberg, but it was a center for enthusiastic support of the arts and by 1927 it harbored a resident artist, Augustus F. "Gus" Kenderdine, who occupied a studio at the top of the Physics Building. A colorful personality, Gus, who had been trained in Manchester and in Paris, had come to Saskatchewan in 1907, settled on a ranch at Lashburn and made Saskatoon his urban home.

Like the traditionalists of Ontario, Kenderdine tended to see his environment with an English vision. He was attracted to the parklands and to the North more than to the open plains. His paintings of the Emma Lake environs where he later conducted a summer school for the university reflect the quality of the northern woods.

There was also an active Art Society in the city, and while the paintings in many homes were likely to be of sheep — not cows, for Saskatonians were not so wealthy as Montrealers — there was a growing interest in local and Canadian originals.

Bob Hurley and Eddie Dawe saw nothing in Saskatoon to make them want to hang up their hats and call it home, and certainly they weren't interested in art. They went to a few shows; they had a choice of three motion picture houses and there was also the Empire Theatre where touring companies from Britain brought live theater and vaudeville to the outposts of Empire. When their taste for city lights had been satisfied, Bob and Eddie turned their attention to investigating job opportunities. They heard that homesteads were still available in the North, and with visions of becoming independent landowners, decided to file in the White Fox district, north of Tisdale, in the northeast. They bought some winter clothing and packs, and took the Tisdale train. From Tisdale they went by truck to Nipawin where they filed papers and paid their ten-dollar fees. Maps showed them that their holdings were in a heavily forested area of white poplar up to ten inches in diameter, mixed with swamp willow and white birches. Realizing that some experience in a lumber camp would be valuable before they started to clear their land, they went off to try their luck at getting work in a camp.

The lumbering territory at that time was a wilderness of spruce forest, with tamarack, birch, and balsam mixed in. From Nipawin to The Pas was about 125 miles, with camps at ten- to fifteen-mile intervals, close to the river where the cut logs were stacked on the ice ready for the spring drive to The Pas (Plate VII). There was only one road, known as the tote road, and the company truck at Nipawin went only as far as the first camp. With

Logs piled on the river bank at his first lumber camp

their packs strapped to their shoulders they hiked to the next camp where "Old Jones" was the chief and Hector McLeod the foreman. After the ten-mile walk, no wonder Bob remembered the meal they were given: stewed beef, boiled potatoes, cabbage, two kinds of pickles, ketchup, lots of fresh bread, hot biscuits, all the apple or raisin pie they could eat, and "C.P.R. strawberries" (stewed prunes).

Bob's job was on the ice, chopping up and burning brush; Eddie worked on the river bank, excavating tree stumps. After two days, Eddie was fired, so the pair walked on to the next camp, which was the hospital camp. The hospital had been completed, but several log huts for storage and equipment were being built. Bill McLaren, the boss, hired them. Bob's first job was thawing river clay and mixing it with moss to form a mortar to fill in the chinks between the logs; then his job was the getting of balsam trees; then cutting ice blocks for the ice pit. About mid-February, Eddie was fired again. Bob stayed on, and his final job was going with a portable mechanical log saw to isolated camps and cutting up vast piles of dried spruce windfalls for fuel.

When the spring thaw came, he collected his pay slip and trudged to The Pas. His pay was thirty dollars a month, less one dollar a month for hospital fees and laundry charges, and less the price of the moccasins, mitts, rubbers, cigarettes, paper, and stamps for which he had signed. He joyfully boarded a train, and at that moment banished all thought of proving up his 160 acres of white poplar.

He had been back in Saskatoon for a week, staying at the YMCA, when he met Johnny Drayton, who had been the water teamster at Plato. Drayton introduced him to Billy Hill, of Hill's Nursery, at his store opposite the Hudson's Bay Company on Second Avenue. Mr. Hill owned a ten-acre plot at South Saskatoon near the C.N.R. water tower and coal dock, a district known as Grasswood; in 1972, it is the built-up district of Avalon waiting for a multi-million-dollar shopping mall. Mr. Hill needed a man to water the plants and to weed out the pigweed and Russian thistle. Hurley worked there till mid-July and left with a promise of work for the next spring. Some dozen years later, he made sketches of the tower and coal dock, a few years before they were razed.

In the meantime, Bob had made a new friend, Fred Miller, of Lancashire, and they decided to hike across the prairie and look for farm work. They took a streetcar to the city's western limits and then walked along the railway track. They were plagued by mosquitoes when they tried to sleep and scorched by the midsummer sun as they walked. Having neglected to carry any water or fruit, they were parched to a point of desperation before they came to the first farm within sight of the tracks. No one was home, so they drank from the horse trough and saw, after they had quenched their thirst, that there were two dead hens in the water. They were only glad that they hadn't seen them before they drank. When they reached Milden, they treated themselves to a bed and bought some provisions, including oranges.

From Milden, they followed dirt or gravel roads, sometimes cutting across pastures or fields of summerfallow. They would walk for a few miles, then rest and suck at an orange, and Bob would make music on his harmonica. At last, as they traveled over a slightly hilly region, they saw elevators in the distance, which they identified from their map as the elevators of Greenan. Noticing a few farm buildings in a ravine and hearing the sound of water being pumped, they followed their ears until they came upon a man watering his five-horse team. He introduced himself as Jack Gibbs and took them to meet his older brother George with whom he operated a mixed farm.

The Gibbs brothers engaged Bob and Fred at a dollar a day plus keep until harvest time, when they would pay higher wages. Bob's job was to build a scaffold and paint the large two-story house. The two lonely bachelor farmers who had come from England some years before and the two itinerant hired hands who had been in Canada only a year got on well together, and after the harvesting was done, they played host at a neighborhood party. As his contribution to the entertainment, Bob, dressed as a ghost and dragging a logging chain, acted and sang an old song he had learned from his father, with the refrain —

For I'm the ghost of John James Christopher Benjamin Binns,
I was cut down, right in midst of my sins.
Oh, my home is down below,
I'm let out for an hour or so.
When the cock begins to crow
Farewell Benjamin Binns.

At "cock crow" he let out such an effective and piercing rooster scream that one of the ladies in the gathering fainted. Shades of his uncle Alfred and his brother Charlie and the good old English music hall!

Fred Miller went back to England; Hurley decided to go north for the winter and he found work in Old Jones's camp, with Hector McLeod still the foreman. He worked as a limber with a saw gang, his particular job being to strip the limbs from the trees, after ten or fifteen had been cut, and to pile the limbs and burn them.

At Christmas, a sentimental time for Bob, the lumberjacks had roast beef as the main dinner dish, with special plum pudding for dessert plus cake with colored icing, mince pie, and freshly baked gingerbread. The men spent the afternoon reading, writing letters, smoking, talking, playing cards, or just plain loafing. In the evening they put on a concert, with Jones, Hector, and the timekeeper as honored guests. The concert was staged in the roomy utility area that joined the two long sections of the bunkhouse. There was a band composed of a mandolinist, a fiddler, Hurley with meat bones as percussion gadgets and his harmonica, and "Sheffield" Tom who did tricky things with the cutlery. A tap-dancing act, lively tunes on a squeeze-box, and a show of wrist wrestling completed the entertainment card. And they all sang.

"Except for very cold days," Hurley recalled years later, "life in the bush was enjoyable, particularly on days when the sun brightened the depths of the woods creating magical patterns of blue snow shadows, and illuminating the varied green hues of the evergreens, and the golden tints of the swamp willows."

He had been in the habit of sketching camp scenes to include in letters to his family and friends in England and he found that he had begun to enjoy sketching for the sake of sketching, matching his skill against an ever-widening variety of subjects. In February, 1925, he sent to Winnipeg for a box of water colors and some paper. One fine Sunday morning he sat on a butter box sketching the buildings against a background of dark spruce and white poplar. Old Jones stopped, looked, and uttered a grunt of approval. Bob was delighted — and he has always been delighted by approval.

Back in Saskatoon, which had become his headquarters between jobs, he stayed at the "Y" for a week, enjoying the attractions of city life — a shower, meals of his own choosing for which he frequented Collier's Cafe on Second Avenue, shows, and a vaudeville at the Empire Theatre — it could have been the famous "Dumbbells" that he saw, for those World War I veterans toured Canada annually with their popular variety show, playing before packed houses. To an Englishman like Hurley, nourished on the repertoire of the music hall, attendance at a vaudeville would be as welcome as a drink of water after a long, hot, dusty walk, even with dead hens in the trough.

Again he went to work for Mr. Hill at Grasswood, living in a shack on the property. Again he went harvesting in the fall. Again he returned to the Saskatoon "Y" and there he had a reunion with Eddie Dawe who had been working as a porter in the Flanagan Hotel on 21st Street at Third Avenue (now the Senator).

The work that Hurley had found in the camps and on the farms involved hard manual labor. Bob was tall and wiry, and at that time had energy to spare, but nevertheless he had found the work pretty backbreaking. While he had been attracted to country jobs ever since he had started his working life, he had also tired of them rather quickly, having found the leisure time very boring with no choice of books to keep him company. He had been in Canada a little over two years, and as he looked back on them the great adventure took the shape of a monotonous repetition of poorly paid, routine jobs, offering no promise or challenge of any kind.

The experiences had been endurable, sometimes even enjoyable, because they had been new. But the novelty was wearing off, and still he had no idea of what he wanted to do or what he wanted to be. Better to be with a family who cared than among strangers who drifted in the same boat. He began to feel about the Canada he had encountered as Samuel Butler had felt about Montreal when he had exclaimed, O God — O Montreal! — O God — O Canada! Surely there was more to life than hard work for bosses who didn't give a damn for anything except the almighty dollar! That was the mood Hurley was in when he met Eddie Dawe, and Dawe being of similar mind, the two decided to work their way back to England as tenders on a cattle boat.

They had heard that by paying a five-dollar fee to the stock shipper at South Saskatoon, he would assure an official pass on the nightly stock train, the 404. They paid the fee, but received no pass, and the conductor bumped them between Nokomis and Leross. They walked to Leross, shipped their luggage to Winnipeg and took the train to Melville. And there, by a chance that wasn't too surprising in the twenties when itinerant workers had a sort of brotherhood society like that of hobos, they met Mike Shea, who had worked at Plato when they had. Mike was an expert at riding the rails illegally, and under his guidance they boarded the 404 by slipping through a trap door near the roof and lying flat on the feed racks above a carload of Hereford steers pulling out mouthfuls from the men's hay-padded couch.

Bob and Eddie got off for food when the train stopped for water, and when it started without them, they jumped on a flatcar loaded with telephone poles and had a scary, chilly ride until they were chased off at Rivers, Manitoba. A kind-hearted official let them ride in the end caboose, warning them to make themselves scarce before the train reached Winnipeg.

At Winnipeg they took a room in the Salvation Army hostel for twenty-five cents a night, and found a cafe where they could get a full-course dinner for the same amount. Still anxious to get to England, they visited the stock-yards. Bob was offered a stockman's pass for Weiller and Williams to travel with stock to Boston, but as there was no second pass for Eddie, he chose to stay with his friend.

As the lice were bad at the "Sally Anne" and the rats kept them awake at night with the racket they made in the garbage cans, they found accommodation in a rooming house east of Main. It happened to be a house in the district recently described by James Gray in *Red Lights on the Prairies* (Macmillans, Toronto, 1971), but they minded their own business, others minded theirs, and occasionally they all met for a friendly game of bridge. During the time Bob and Eddie stayed there, they took out library cards and spent a good deal of time reading, they attended shows, and went, once, to a Pentecostal Mission — for a lark. They celebrated New Year's day at their favorite cafe with turkey, vegetables, and plum pudding, all for fifty cents.

In February they got work at Vassar, seventy-five miles from Winnipeg, cutting and stacking tamarack for a French settler at seventy-five cents a cord. It was hard-earned money, for the work of felling a tree, cutting it into four-foot logs, and stacking the logs into eight-foot piles was the hardest Hurley had yet done. They were lucky if they made a dollar a day in excess of costs, although they were told that some Swedes who had done similar work had made up to six dollars a day.

The stand of tamarack, mixed with spruce and cedar, was at a lake area a few miles away from the Frenchman's home farm. Eddie and Bob were joined by another Englishman by the name of Harry, and they shared a ten-by-six-foot cabin with a dirt floor, hay-filled beds, a dilapidated cookstove, and a heater. They cut moss and chinked up the holes in the walls, swept out the litter, and settled in to batch it. Eddie and Harry supplied dried firewood for cooking and heating; Bob did the cooking, with the aid of a "Blue Ribbon" cookbook. Their mainstay was sourdough biscuits, which Eddie called "Hurley Ammunition." They missed the comforts of a company camp, but enjoyed the freedom of being on their own.

They cut trees from dawn to dusk and barely made enough to pay for their supplies, brought weekly by their employer, the mending of ax handles, and the sharpening of saws. By the first of March they had cut most of the tamarack, so they cut spruce for pulpwood and cedars for posts until the term of their employment was over at the end of March.

Eddie joined a local army unit in Winnipeg; Harry went East to look for work; Bob, after a short stint with a mean farmer who had a mean bull, neither of whom he liked, found a job with the Canadian National Railway at a small place called Quibell in northern Ontario, a rocky area dotted with lakes. One of his jobs was to operate a pumpcar and inspect the tracks for miles on either side of Quibell in anticipation of the passing of the phantom-like silk train with its perishable cargo of raw silk (cocoons with live silkworms inside). The C.N.R. picked up the bales from Japan in Vancouver and sped them across the country to New York via Toronto and Buffalo. "The fastest passenger train time," writes Ken Liddell in *I'll Take the Train,* "from Vancouver to Buffalo was 107 hours, but the silk trains made it in 74 hours and 50 minutes. Every minute counted." (Prairie Books, Western Producer, Saskatoon, 1966.) And well it might, as the value of the cargo was usually around $5,000,000. In 1927, the longest silk train moved by the Canadian National comprised twenty-one cars carrying 7,200 bales worth $7,000,000. So Bob's inspection was no routine task.

Hurley found the Quibell environment attractive and he would often wander along the tracks with his sketch pad, but when he would stop and try to record his impressions the deerflies and the mosquitoes soon had him on the move again. Only the Indians who gathered the abundant blueberries seemed impervious to the insect attacks; or perhaps Ole, a Swedish squatter who specialized in making homebrew, when he had had enough of his hootch, a commodity he was always ready to share.

It was at Quibell that Hurley painted his first on-the-spot water color, a small picture (four and a half by six and a half) showing the Red Cross hospital with a suggestion of the rocks and stunted evergreens extending beyond the building complex, and with a sky that hints at Hurley's later preoccupation with sky effects. The picture is interesting because of its early date in his career and because it was painted before he knew any of the fundamentals of water-color technique (plate VIII).

By August Bob had had enough of Quibell and its bugs and the type of labor involved at a railway divisional point, and he decided to return to Western Canada. Unable to find a city job, after he had rested up and bought some new clothing, he shipped out to work on the farm of Kim Bole at Elfros, about 125 miles east of Saskatoon. Mr. Bole operated a large mixed farm with dairy and beef cattle, large flocks of turkeys and hens, and a prosperous egg sideline. The daughter was the cook, Mrs. Bole was the poultry expert; Mr. Bole ran the market garden; the son, with Hurley and another hired man, did the usual hard farm labor. His stay at the Bole farm was pleasant, but not pleasant enough for him to accept the permanent work he was offered. He was still a rolling stone, never satisfied for long at one place. While at Elfros, he bought a set of oil paints, but quickly decided that oil was not his medium. He simply could not achieve the effects with oils that he wished. Twenty years or so later, he thought he might like oils, but he had to forego the medium because of the time involved.

Mr. Hurley went from farm to camp to farm. During the summer of 1928 he helped Johnny Drayton with gardening jobs in Saskatoon and as Mr. Drayton's work became more demanding, he assumed full responsibility for several of the jobs. In the fall he went to the employment agency and was approached by a farmer looking for harvest help. Their meeting, Hurley later thought, was a miracle of the same sort that had directed him to Canada. The farmer, George Young, invited Hurley to drive back with him to his farm at Ruthilda, about one hundred miles west of Saskatoon. On the way they stopped for lunch, and much to Hurley's surprise, Mr. Young said grace. Hurley hadn't heard grace since the days when his mother had tried to give her children a modicum of religious background by seeing that they said their prayers and by observing such customs as saying grace and singing hymns. His life in Canada, particularly in the lumber camps, had been rough and ready, the language of the swearing and cursing variety, and any religious observances had belonged, like women, to another world.

Hurley's surprise at hearing grace, however, was nothing compared to his astonishment the following morning when he went to the farm kitchen for breakfast and heard Mrs. Young ask, "Who's going to do the reading this morning?" Then they all dropped to their knees to listen to the daily text. Hurley knelt with them, thinking that it was at any rate a new experience and one which he might be able to use if he ever decided to write about his adventures.

Whatever their religious convictions — he discovered they belonged to the Holiness Movement, a branch of the Methodist faith — the family was the kindest of any he had met in Canada and treated him like one of themselves, never as a hired hand.

He returned to Saskatoon after harvesting and thought he had broken the pattern of lumber camps in the winter and farms and gardens in the summer when he found employment at Eaton's. The T. Eaton Company, which had operated a warehouse and mail-order business for a number of years in Saskatoon, had bought the F. R. MacMillan department store in 1927 and had conducted the business on its premises (now the Avenue Building) until their new store was ready for occupancy. The "new" store, now called the "old" building from the eminence of Eaton's present location in Saskatoon's attractive Midtown Plaza, was opened with a flourish on December the fifth, 1928, in time for the Christmas shopping rush. It was in this store that Hurley had his first white-collar job, and he bought a twenty-dollar gray tweed suit in order to look presentable.

He took his breakfast and evening meal at the Canada Cafe near his rooming house on Avenue B north. The cafe was owned by Chinese whose custom it was to provide free Christmas and New Year's dinners to their clientele. Hurley took advantage of their generosity and relished his Christmas dinner of turkey and the trimmings. He hadn't realized that his job was only for the Christmas season, and when he received his walking ticket before New Year's, he felt that he was once again a failure.

If anyone could have told him that in the 1950's Lady Eaton would be presented with a Hurley water color on the occasion of her visit to the Saskatoon store after the publication of her memoirs, he would have treated his informer as he had treated the inmates of the asylum at Shewsbury — as a person to avoid.

Hurley took advantage of the complimentary New Year's dinner at the Canada Cafe, but somehow it wasn't quite so tasty as his Christmas meal. However, he was grateful for it. The Chinese custom, he thought later when he and his family spent more than eight years on relief, was one that others might well emulate. The only Christmas hamper the Hurleys received when on relief came from an organization referred to by their temperance friends as "the drunken Legion." Mr. Hurley was an ex-serviceman; Mrs. Hurley was a homemaker who had learned the hard way how to manage on the proverbial shoestring. They had their own opinion of the Legion, and it wasn't modified by an abusive adjective.

Bob did what he had done every winter he had been in Canada. He found a job in a lumber camp. He sold his cheap tweed suit, put his bush clothes in his pack, and headed north for work, through Melfort, Tisdale, and Crooked River to Mistatim, thinking that 1929 was starting out even less favorably than had 1926 when he had had to give up the idea of getting back to England.

The Carrot, Swan, and Crooked rivers converged at Mistatim, and the camp was in the center. At the first thaw it became an icy-cold swamp. Dispirited, weakend by a bout with the 'flu, tired of knocking about, he wrote to the Youngs and asked if they could use him as a permanent hired man. They could; and in April he went back to Ruthilda.

"I know now," he wrote in 1966, "an unknown force was guiding me into an entirely new phase of life."

The Youngs made him feel at home immediately, and he joined in their family activities and observances. True to their convictions, they tried to influence him in a religious manner, but he remained an unresponsive subject.

He remained unresponsive until mid-July. One Sunday, the family, with Hurley, drove over to nearby Herschel to attend Gospel meetings. During the morning session Bob dozed most of the time, only vaguely aware of what was taking place. At the evening session, however, Beulah Argue, who was conducting the service (her brother, Watson Argue, is a prominent evangelist now preaching in San Diego), asked him up in the choir. As he enjoyed group singing, he willingly complied but felt no urge to identify himself with the group.

On Monday, a hot, sultry day, he was harrowing with five horses when a thunderstorm developed. The horses became restive, so he took them home early and went to his bunkhouse to wait the call for supper. He began thinking about the hymns he had sung the night before and wondering if there were anything to the whole performance that he hadn't been able to comprehend. He would pray, he decided, and ask God, if there was a God, to give him a sign. Mrs. Young had presented him with a copy of the New Testament, and he felt compelled to open it at random. He received his message:

Jesus saith unto him, Thomas, because thou hast seen me, thou hast believed: blessed are they that have not seen, and yet have believed.

And many other signs truly did Jesus in the presence of his disciples, which are not written in this book:

But these are written, that ye might believe that Jesus is the Christ, the Son of God; and that believing ye might have life through his name.

John 20: 29-31

When he read those words, he felt a sensation like a bolt of lightning pass through him. In that instant, he was Born Again! He was thirty-five years old.

From then on he started reading all the material available about his new faith. He found much to support him in *The Golden Grain* by Dr. Charles S. Price, in the many scriptural magazines which the Youngs received, and of course, in the Holy Bible, particularly the book of Daniel.

He stayed with the Youngs for harvesting and through the winter months. He sent away for a guitar, taught himself to play — he couldn't then, and still can't, read a note of music — and became proficient enough that he was able to play with a gospel orchestra.

Mr. Hurley returned to Saskatoon in the spring of 1930, for the Youngs were beginning to feel the financial pinch of the world-wide depression that had struck in October of 1929, and one of his first acts was to seek baptism at Elim Pentecostal Tabernacle at 25th Street and Avenue A (now Idylwyld Drive). According to their custom, baptism was by complete submersion in a tank. In the baptismal waters he was cleansed of the sins and the errors of his old way of life and of thinking, and he emerged a new man.

Far from harboring any thoughts about returning to England, he was firmly convinced then that his decision to emigrate to Canada had been divinely inspired. O God — O Canada! became not a comment on the futility of his life in the New World as it had been when he had felt that Canada had nothing to offer him, but a sort of prayer thanking God for having directed his steps to Canada, to Saskatchewan, to Ruthilda, and to the True Faith.

Elevators at Sutberland

1950. 12 x 10"

4

Religion at the Center

AFTER ROBERT HURLEY'S religious awakening he saw the world in general and his world in particular as a Fundamentalist, accepting the literal interpretation of the Bible, rejecting evolution, vehemently believing his religion to be the only path to salvation. Magazines, pamphlets, and tracts abound explaining the main principles and minute details of Fundamentalism, which is not exclusive to any one sect but is followed, with variations, by most of the off-shoot groups from the "established" Church. A general survey of the main characteristics of ten of the larger sects is given by G. W. Target in *Under the Christian Carpet* (Clifton Books, London, 1969); and an anthropological, psychological, and sociological analysis of religious protest movements, including an account of the recent rise of sects in the United States, is provided by J. Milton Yinger in *The Scientific Study of Religion* (The Macmillan Company, New York, 1970). For the initiate and for the curious there is no end to the amount of material existing on religious experiences. What is relevant to Mr. Hurley's story is not an explanation of his religion *per se,* but a brief review of its effects on his life.

Within the boundaries of Fundamentalism, Mr. Hurley is interdenominational. He attended services at Elim Tabernacle for several months; he often played his guitar on the platform, and he designed and painted a ten-foot-high sign for the Christmas program — JESUS SAVES. In company with some ex-servicemen whom he met at the Legion, he also worshiped at the Apostolic Mission on 19th Street and Avenue G, and when they were being baptized, he was baptized for a second time, again by complete submersion. He subscribed to the beliefs of the British-Israel World Federation; he sanctioned the teachings of the Plymouth Brethren, which his wife and children followed: he frequently attended the Salvation Army Citadel; and always on Sundays he listened to the Word over the radio. Visiting revivalists and evangelists often had Mr. Hurley as a member of their audiences.

The diaries which Mr. Hurley kept for 1938 and from 1950 to 1958 inclusive are packed with religious observations on every subject and activity that came within his range. It would be a mistake, however, to judge him solely by what he wrote in the diaries, for he was often so swept away by what he had just heard or read that he tended to quote the source rather than to express his own opinions. To get a balanced picture of the man it is best to dilute his written statements, which are often vituperative, breathing hell-fire and damnation to Communists and Catholics in tune with Pentecostal or Apostolic preachings. In the give-and-take of conversation, and in his correspondence, the loving, forgiving aspect of Christianity is most often to the fore. If one were to know Robert Hurley only through his diaries, one would be inclined to label him as a bigot and a man of strange contradictions. Persons who have had the good fortune to know him, as an associate or a friend, or even casually, think of him in the main as a gentle and genuinely humble man, kind, generous, and pretty tolerant of human weaknesses.

Although almost constant physical discomfort or pain has at times brought him to the edge of despair, he is essentially a blithe spirit, with an engaging, childlike enthusiasm. He is a simple person with a single-mindedness about many things. It is not impossible to interpret his single-mindedness as selfishness or obstinacy, but it would be wrong to claim selfishness or obstinacy as intentional. His religious conversion helped him to develop the strength to endure hardship, the ability to accept misfortune, and the determination to serve truth and beauty. That it made him also stern in his attitude to frivolity, impatient with the tinsel of the entertainment world, and rigid in his opinion about other religions and beliefs, was part and parcel of the teachings he accepted.

On the superficial level, he gave up smoking and drinking, although he had never indulged in either to any great extent; he ceased the swearing and cursing of camp language; he turned his back on movies and plays and certain sports, particularly on any that involved a degree of brutality, such as wrestling and boxing. In short, he renounced the so-called worldly pleasures in favor of seeking spiritual peace.

"I find prayer or meditating on the Lord even more necessary than bread, drink or sleep," was how he summed up his source of joy and contentment in this world. His idea of Hell was "to have to listen to a hockey broadcast, or be subjected to Idle Gossip, Foolish Light Chatter, or be tortured by jazz."

It became his custom to rise early and to spend some time meditating on the Lord. There is constant reference in the diaries to "meditating," "waiting on the Lord," "making contact," "feeling the peace of the Lord." There were times when he wasn't successful in making contact, times when he felt too ill and tired to pray with fervor or to attend church, but he recognized those times as being "a real test of faith." "God," he wrote, "withholds His help in order to discipline His children." He firmly believed that "God alone can heal," and on occasion he went to church to be anointed with oil at the altar and to have the elders say a healing prayer.

After demobilization, when he had been staying with his sister Margaret at the old home on Oakfield Road, he had contracted a virulent type of influenza, which had weakened his lungs and left him with a chronic nasal and throat infection. From then on, increasingly in later years, he was tormented by a sinus condition, severe leg cramps, an allergic skin condition, boils, and general debility. Almost as numerous as the references to religion in his diaries are his references to poor health. Frequently, he had to take a few days of sick leave from work. When being anointed with oil didn't heal his boils, he called on his doctor for help. An injection of one of the new wonder drugs did the trick — God healed in one way or another.

By 1955, his physical condition was causing him almost constant distress and misery. A series of X-rays revealed nothing. In June he was diagnosed as having acute anemia, and he took a ten-day sick leave, which extended to five weeks.

Scarcely had he returned to his job when he was taken suddenly ill one Sunday and had to be rushed to the hospital. It was discovered that a small tumor was blocking the passing of urine, and he underwent surgery on August the thirtieth. From then until March the twentieth, 1956, when he was certified free of cancer, he lived under its shadow. In 1969 he was hospitalized for a second time for a heart condition. In 1972, he was in the hospital again for a gall bladder operation. He has endured countless hours of illness, and has been helped to accept them by his belief in a divine guiding power — and by medical science. God sorely tested his faith, and didn't find it wanting.

In accordance with the precepts of his faith, Mr. Hurley has been an evangelist and a witness. On November the twenty-second, 1951, for instance, he mailed out twenty-five copies of the gospel booklet "The Reason Why" to university contacts and close friends "in the hope that something will be done to further the harvesting of God's precious grain." On the twenty-eighth, he sent an additional eighteen letters and books as witness to the Gospel, commenting in his diary: "We sow the seed but only the Lord can give the increase. Most of these university contacts are non-churchgoers, atheists and skeptics so the need is great."

It was not his style to knock on doors or to force his opinions on unwilling listeners, but when sufficiently provoked, he would not hesitate to speak out, as on the day he "rebuked a vile foul-mouthed sinner for using the precious name of Jesus as a swear word," and on the occasion when he "stirred up a hornet's nest in protesting at work on the sin and brutality of sport," becoming "quite fiery" in his denunciation of sin.

"It seems God smiled on my efforts," he told his diary at the end of the hornet's nest day. At one o'clock a doctor and his wife called to buy a water color; at five o'clock a minister dropped in to buy another; and by mail, an official of the dairy association in Regina requested a painting for a gift to a distinguished visitor. When he went home, he learned that son Chuck, after six weeks of unemployment, had started work that day with the Saskatchewan Power Corporation.

He was often awed by God's answers to his prayers and good works. In the early 1930's when he was sharing digs with a carpenter friend and they were desperate for funds, he suggested that they pray for help. Two days later he received a check for sixty dollars, delayed payment for harvesting work done the previous fall. During a convention of Apostolic Churches in 1954, he gave a cash donation of twenty-five dollars and offered to board one missionary. The next day he received seventy-five dollars from the Teachers College for three water colors. "The Lord," he wrote, "already has sent good interest." The same sort of experience happened time after time.

As an expression of his gratitude for having been born again, for receiving evidences of God's concern for him, for achieving success in his career, he gladly gave his witness. On October the thirty-first, 1952, he wrote that he had spent all the forenoon composing a manuscript to send to a Christian association in Toronto. "I thought it time to get my testimony in circulation," he penned, "as to the wonderful way the Lord changed me from a failure and infidel to a place of success and faith."

A more or less inevitable result of his religious conversion was a loss of interest in mundane affairs, or perhaps more accurately, a shifting of emphasis in his attitude to the affairs of this world, including ordinary social intercourse. He deplored civilized man's "frantic struggle for pleasure, wealth or prestige," ignoring the fact, even though he himself had had to accept relief for many years, that the great majority of men are primarily concerned with making ends meet. He avoided, whenever possible, picnics and parties, although he enjoyed entertaining friends in his own home and was always an affable and generous host. After one social call, he wrote that he considered "listening to light trivial social talk a lost evening," and that he had found the conversation on "about the level of an inmate of a mental home." Not all gatherings and parties were "lost evenings," however, for on more than one occasion he noted that he had made a valuable contact.

Because civilized man was too busy in the pursuit of pleasure and wealth, and because all other religious beliefs were "satanic and conceived in Hell's pit," Mr. Hurley looked about him at "a sin-sick world that has lost its way." He frequently referred to his belief that civilization was on the verge of another Armageddon, and he listed "signs of the soon coming of the 'Day of the Lord' — Italy — floods. Sicily — volcanic activity. Far East — famine, war. Nation rising against nation — earthquakes, political chaos. God is surely laying on the rod of correction to the nations." This was in 1951.

According to Mr. Target in *Under the Christian Carpet,* the sects are in agreement about the Second Coming of Christ, but they differ widely in their opinions of how the Battle of Armageddon will develop and when. The Church of God has established October the seventh, 1975, as the date for the Second Coming, a date also favored by Jehovah's Witnesses and by Herbert W. Armstrong's "Radio Church of God." The sects which favor this date put great faith in the prophecies in the Book of Daniel. On the other hand, the British-Israelites, who in addition to their interpretations from the Bible base their prophecies on the Great Pyramid of Cheops at Gizah, have chosen the date of September the seventeenth, 2001. Mr. Hurley has no doubt about the soon coming of the Day of Judgment, but believes it unscriptural to determine a date.

A man's religion cannot be contained in a few words. If he is as fervent a believer as Mr. Hurley, his religious convictions permeate everything he does and all that he thinks and feels. As an artist, Hurley is not only expressing his faith in a Divine Guiding Power, but he is also serving his God by witnessing to the wonders He has created. His painting is a form of prayer.

The Hurley one meets in the diaries, so often calling on the wrath of God to destroy a wicked and corrupt world, so intolerant of others' beliefs and customs, and the Hurley one meets in person, so devoted in his pursuit of truth and beauty, so hospitable to all callers, seem sometimes like two different persons. They aren't; they are only the expression of two sides of Fundamentalism. And Hurley is, above all else, a Fundamentalist.

Houses at Twilight

1949. 8½ x 5¼"

5

Saskatoon Becomes Home

IT WAS A CONFIDENT Bob Hurley who returned to Saskatoon in 1930. Happy as he had been on the farm at Ruthilda, feeling his way in the new-found religion, still he had missed city living, particularly the facilities of a well-stocked library. At thirty-five, life had become for him, for the first time, a wonderful experience. He was convinced that with the Lord on his side he would find his way in the world. All doubts had vanished.

Mr. Hurley might not have felt so sanguine had he been able to peer into the economic future of the country, for the depression and the terrible drought conditions, which were to last for a good ten years on the Prairies, had settled in. Whatever was in store for him, however, could not have seemed so frightful and horrible as his life had been during the three years before he had emigrated to Canada, when he had been the victim of his own black depression. In 1930 he saw those early years as a testing time and his decision to emigrate not as a desperate choice between complete failure and possible opportunity but as a divinely directed move. Since he could not peer into the future, he faced it with faith and a renewed sense of adventure, far greater than he had felt in 1923.

In 1928 he had done some gardening jobs for Johnny Drayton and on his own; he decided to follow up the contacts he had made at that time. He basked in his new-found optimism, which matched the optimism of 1928 when the Prairies were not a "next year" land. "This year" had certainly been good enough, and nothing but expansion had been in sight.

Saskatoon, in 1928, was a bustling, prosperous community, reflecting the national, and especially the agricultural, climate — the farmers were preparing to harvest the biggest wheat crop to date, three hundred and twenty-one million bushels. The demand for farm machinery, home appliances and furniture, automobiles, and building materials contributed to a flourishing business life. The largest industry established during the decade, the Robin Hood Mills, opened its plant far out on Avenue B, and individual businesses were thriving. Local bank clearings, customs, and postal revenues were rising steadily to reach an unprecedented peak in 1929. In addition to businessmen, professional men benefited from the prosperity. New homes and improvements to existing ones were in vogue. The population had risen from around 25,000 in 1921 to nearly 40,000 by the end of the decade. In 1928 the two daily papers, the *Phoenix* and the *Star,* were amalgamated to form the *Star-Phoenix,* publishing three editions daily. On the sports scene Ethel Catherwood was the heroine of the year and was given a royal welcome home after setting a new record for the ladies' running high jump at the Olympics. (Facts and figures about Saskatoon are taken from *The Saskatoon Story, Up the years from the Temperance Colony*, 1882-1952, by Bruce Peel and Eric Knowles, privately printed, 1952.)

Saskatoon, which Robert Hurley grew to know like the palm of his hand, was an attractive city built on both sides of the winding, swift-flowing South Saskatchewan River; that is, it was swift-flowing until the construction of the Gardiner Dam in 1967, about seventy miles south of Saskatoon, turned it into a shadow of its former mighty self.

Most of the residences of the more affluent families had been located not far from the river banks, and the natural growth of willows, chokecherries, wild roses, and saskatoon bushes had been fitted into garden plots and spacious lawns, with quick-growing caragana hedges, butternut trees, cottonwoods, and elms adding to the parklike effect, unusual for a prairie town.

The majority of the homes had been erected during the early boom days from 1910 to 1913. If there had been a city planner, perhaps he could have saved more of the bush-covered high banks for public enjoyment. The city fathers, in 1907, had reluctantly allowed Spadina Crescent West to be ruined for residential or park purposes by agreeing to construction of railway tracks near the river. They hadn't seen fit, however, to prevent the building of private homes along the top of the bank where Saskatchewan Crescent now curves. The homeowners had exclusive riverside lots — not always to their advantage, as the proximity of the river made the lots dangerous play areas for children and as the river, more than a few times, flooded landscaped terraces. However, the area granted to private owners was not extensive, and in the eastern side of the city, the homes were built back of the river, allowing for future footpaths and drives along the river banks. Spadina Crescent East and Saskatchewan Crescent East became attractive residential areas, while the natural beauty of the banks were retained for the enjoyment of the public. With commendable foresight, the city fathers reserved extensive areas for future park and playground development.

Saskatchewan Crescent West and Poplar Crescent, curving parallel to it, were known as the Idylwyld district. No Indian chiefs lived there, but doctors, lawyers, bankers, and what today would be called "executives" populated the charming area. It was in Idylwyld that Mr. Hurley began his gardening career. As he became better known, he was offered work beyond Broadway Avenue along Saskatchewan Crescent East as far as Clarence Avenue, and then, across the University, or 25th Street, Bridge, along Spadina Crescent East. The river bank, indeed, became his sidewalk. Just

Saskatoon, c. 1954, showing its bridges, the course of the river through the city, and some of the regions frequented by Hurley as he worked as a gardener or took sketching trips

1. Goldeye Bay
2. C.P.R. Bridge
3. Spadina Crescent East
4. University Bridge
5. Broadway Bridge
6. 19th Street (Traffic) Bridge
7. Technical Collegiare
8. City Power House, 100 yards to left
9. Robin Hood Mill
10. C.N.R. Bridge
11. Idylwyld District (Sask. & Poplar Cres.)
12. Exhibition Grounds Area
13. G.T.P. Bridge (now C.N.R.)
14. Site of Queen Elizabeth Power House
15. Yorath Island

as he had enjoyed the sights and sounds of London as he had walked from Mark Lane to Shoe Lane, so he took in the sights and sounds of Saskatoon as he walked along the banks of its river from one job to another. The river became, and remained, an important element in his life.

Saskatchewan summers are short; the winters long. It was not possible for Mr. Hurley to make enough money from gardening to tide him over the winter. For several weeks one winter he worked near Langham, about thirty miles west of Saskatoon, on the dairy farm of Larry Crick, whom he had met at the Elim Tabernacle. And the delayed payment for harvesting which came as an answer to his prayers helped him and his friend through part of the next winter. Also, he enrolled with the unemployed ex-servicemen at the Legion and was provided with two meals a day. To keep fit they would go for workouts at the YMCA. As the depression deepened, the Idylwyld crescents became known as Mortgage lanes, but Mr. Hurley had made good friends in the district and while the people couldn't pay him much, he still found work here and there and he was able to stretch the dollars and the dimes further and further as prices fell.

Building permits in Saskatoon in 1929 had reached $5,902,123, the highest figure since 1912. Early in the year the new Public Library building on 23rd Street at Fourth Avenue was opened (it was completely rebuilt in 1966) and it was to become not only a haven for Hurley, as it was for many unemployed, but also, in the late 1930's under the direction of James S. Wood, one of Mr. Hurley's first patrons (Plate X). After the October disaster, however, only those buildings which were already under construction or in the blueprint stage were completed. As a Dominion Government relief project, the Broadway Bridge, designed by professors and senior students of the university's College of Engineering, was built, bringing the number of bridges to six — the same number the "City of Bridges" still boasts.

Two of Mr. Hurley's favorite retreats as the thirties advanced were near the Grand Trunk Pacific Bridge (now the Canadian National Railway Bridge) at the southwest limits of the city (Plate XIV), and beyond the Canadian Pacific Railway Bridge at the northeast limits. Bridges became, like the river, a part of his life. When he lived in the downtown area, he had to cross a bridge to get to his jobs in Idylwyld; when he roomed in Nutana (across the bridges from downtown), he had to cross a bridge to get to his jobs on Spadina.

One day, in 1932, when he was watering a lawn on Spadina Crescent, a young woman in maid's uniform wished him a good day from the next-door property. Not long after their casual exchange, Bob boarded a streetcar to go to an event at the Exhibition Grounds and had the pleasure of sharing a seat with the same young woman.

Their friendship blossomed into romance quickly. And why not? She spoke, as she does still, with, particularly to Bob's ears, a delightful Irish lilt, and she had the capacity of her people to enjoy life and its whimsies.

In a few ways Isabella Smyth was the exact opposite of Robert Hurley. As the oldest member of her family, she had emigrated to Canada in 1928 in a sort of make-way gesture for the younger members. She had worked for a time in Winnipeg and had then gone to a farm at Carmen, Manitoba, where she had lived practically as a member of the family for three years until the farmer died. Saddened by his death, she had traveled to Saskatoon where a cousin had settled, and in Saskatoon she entered domestic service. She was not restless, not ever changing jobs, but possessed the will and the strength to make the best of existing conditions, a strength that was to prove of great value during the 1930's and later during times of illness. She came from County Tyrone in northern Ireland; the Irish in Bob had come from County Cork in the south. It was the Irish in them both that they found mutually attractive, and they were sympathetic in their religious outlooks.

The decision to make a go of life together in 1932 might have seemed like a foolhardy one to many, but Isabella and Bob, through familiarity with poverty, had no great fear of it. Greater than any fear of poverty was the fear of the loneliness that it could bring. For that matter, wasn't there a popular saying that kept insisting that two could live as cheaply as one? They set up housekeeping in the Colonial Apartments on 20th Street West, and before their first Christmas together had come along they had settled into waiting for the birth of a child. It was the first home that Robert Hurley had known since he had been a boy — and even then his home life had been under the shadow of his father's addiction. He was supremely happy.

The child, a boy whom they named Charles after Bob's grandfather and father and eldest brother, was born in the spring. After a few weeks, Isabella decided that their rooms in the Colonial Apartments were not very convenient for the purposes of caring for a baby, and they moved to the southern outskirts of town on Victoria Avenue near Ruth Street to a house owned by Johnny Drayton's brother. Here, they could have a garden, and Charles — or "Chuck" as they called him — could have fresh air and sunshine. Here, too, they found they had to go on relief. The gardening jobs in the summer of 1933 had dried up as much as the country had.

The mere fact that they had managed to stay off relief until that summer was a tribute to Bob's acceptance and success as a jobbing gardener and to the kindness of the persons who had kept him working for as long as they had found it possible; and a tribute, too, to Isabella's ability to manage. She could make Irish stews and homemade soups by spending not too many pennies, and she was an expert with her needle.

They were certainly not alone in their need for help. In 1933 there were 1,752 families on relief in Saskatoon, and in 1934, the blackest year, there were 2,049, for a total of 8,000 individuals, or nearly one-fifth of the city's population.

Around that time, when people were trying to make the best of things and were being told by President Roosevelt that there was nothing to fear but fear itself, there was a current song that went like this:

> *Just around the corner,*
> *There's a rainbow in the sky,*
> *So let's have another cup of coffee*
> *And let's have another piece of pie.*

Robert Hurley turned that corner in 1932. He found that rainbow, and like the Irish rover that he was, he followed it looking for the pot of gold at the other end. And the treasure was there, in the form of almost unbelievable success as a water-colorist.

6

Follow the Rainbow

FOR MR. HURLEY, in retrospect, the 1930's were a time of wonder. The unemployment, the worry, the deprivations have faded into the background, and remembered vividly are the new friends and the new interests that he acquired. Life, which had been rather a thin affair for him up to that time, became full of rewarding experiences. He might be as poor as a church mouse in the things of this world, but he was as rich as Croesus in the things that mattered — religion, family, friends, career.

Eddie Dawe, Bob's friend of lumberjack and Winnipeg days, was living in the Colonial Apartments when the Hurleys set up house there. One fine evening Bob and Eddie decided to go for a stroll and to drop in at Open House at the Technical Collegiate Institute, which had been built in 1931-32. Classrooms and workshops were open for inspection, and the public had been invited to take a look at the new kind of technical training that was being offered in the city. One workroom particularly attracted Bob, for students were busy sketching a still-life arrangement under the guidance of a short, stocky instructor with a pronounced German accent. Hurley hung around until the instructor was free and then introduced himself, explaining that he liked drawing as a pastime and had a number of sketches at home. The instructor, whose name was Ernest Lindner, talked to him for some time and invited him to bring his sketches some Saturday evening to the London Block, where he, Mr. Lindner, lived. Mr. Hurley's career as an artist began with that chance encounter, for it was at Mr. Lindner's that he met others who were deeply interested in art, some of whom rapidly became lasting friends.

Up to 1932 the names in the Hurley story are noticeable because of their absence. Except for members of his family, Eddie Dawe's name appears most frequently, and their friendship was of the casual, now-and-then kind. Not long after they met at the Colonial Apartments, Eddie took off for the north again, pursuing his elusive dream of farming. At his request by letter, Hurley sent him a list of times for planting grains and vegetables. The last Hurley heard of him, Eddie had beat his way to the West Coast where he had joined up again.

After 1932 the number of names in the Hurley story becomes increasingly, until finally almost incredibly, large. If it were possible to set them all down alphabetically, the list would resemble a telephone directory for a good-sized town. They range in prominence from the Queen of England to John and Jane Doe; from the Governor General of Canada to the ferryman at Clark's Crossing. If the list were to include every owner of a Hurley painting, it would surprise Mr. Hurley himself, for he has no idea of where a great many of the thousands of pictures he has created have come to rest, except that they are scattered far and wide. Every now and then a friend will tell him about having seen a "Hurley" in an embassy in South America or in a professor's home in Aberdeen, Scotland. For a person who is by nature rather a hermit, who is inclined to avoid people rather than to seek them out, Hurley has had people stream into his life in a fantastic way, particularly in the face of the fact that he was nearly forty when he began to mingle with others.

The upshot of his meeting with Mr. Lindner was that he took some sketches to Lindner's home, was encouraged to continue sketching and painting, and was invited to attend, whenever he wished, Lindner's "Saturday Evenings" — for many years a kind of institution among the artists and art-loving public of the city — and to sit in on Mr. Lindner's classes at the Technical school. Mr. Lindner suggested, too, that Hurley show his work to Kenderdine. Kenderdine, who remained aloof from clubs and gatherings and such, and reserved his opinions for those who attended his classes in his studio in the Physics Building, had little advice to give Mr. Hurley who, of course, had no money to take instruction. Kenderdine's opinion was that if people had talent they didn't need his advice, and if they didn't have talent, they couldn't benefit from his advice. He was a most logical man.

Hurley followed Lindner's advice and kept on sketching, mostly articles around the apartment, such as the teapot. Mrs. Hurley recalls that the night before Charles was born, Bob was so engrossed in sketching parakeets from a book that he was scarcely aware of her plight — one way for an expectant father to calm his own nerves, if not his wife's!

After the Hurleys moved out to what was then the southern outskirts of the city on Victoria Avenue in May, 1933, they were busy setting the place in order and planting and tending a garden. When fall came, Bob became a fairly regular and always welcome visitor at the Technical Collegiate's night sketching class. By the spring of 1934 he had some paintings ready to include in the display of students' work.

In the meantime, he had borrowed from the Public Library *The Technique of Water-Colour Painting* by Leonard Richmond and J. Littlejohns (Sir Isaac Pitman & Sons Limited, London, 1930) and had followed it step by step, doing every exercise not once but many times until he was satisfied that he had mastered all the principles. Using the fundamentals he had learned from the book, he copied one of the finished pictures in it, one of a castle

Bob worked at his technique by painting articles around the house, like this tea kettle

water color

in Toledo, Spain. Richmond and Littlejohns were his teachers, the only ones he ever had.

In developing his own technique, he was following the advice of his teachers, advice which struck a very responsive chord in him:

"While it is true, of course, that the creation of a work of art demands a profound knowledge of nature, it does not follow that the early essays in painting pictures should consist of attempts to copy every intricacy of natural effects. Most painters who have approached the problem unsystematically have begun by crowding and ended by simplifying their palettes. We suggest that the student should begin by learning to control the simplest combinations and proceed, step by step, to the more complicated ones, perfecting his technique as he goes. He will then be more likely to discover that the expression of beauty is not only a matter of imitating superficial facts of nature but of interpreting its deeper qualities. He will not be led away, by concentrating attention upon insignificant details, from the fundamental principles of nature — unity, simplicity, vitality, and repose. He will learn to look at nature in a big way."

So exactly did the authors' opinion about nature and about how the artist should approach nature match Hurley's own opinion that even their warning that the handling of water color was "much more exacting in its difficulties and extensive in its possibilities than any other branch of painting" could only have acted as a spur to his impatience to master the fundamentals.

One day, armed with the assurance that he had practiced enough of the exercises to go off on his own and try an original painting, he walked north on Victoria Avenue, across the Traffic Bridge, turned west and walked under the old C.N.R. Bridge and took up his position near the city's Power House, at the tip of Avenue A. The power house was close to the Technical Collegiate, and Mr. Lindner often sent his day students out to do on-the-spot drawings of its patterned expanse. Hurley did a water-color painting, his first on-the-spot landscape painting since he had left Quibell.

He entered his landscape, along with a still life, in the art display at the Saskatoon Exhibition. His still life, a study of a red geranium and white spiraea, was awarded first prize, which pleased Mrs. Hurley who had rescued the geranium from her neighbor's trash pile to provide her husband with something vivid to paint. Although of a later date, "Still Life" (Plate XI) is a good example of his skill in this genre. His landscape won a third prize, good enough to make him determined to try his hand at landscape painting again.

He was not so jubilant, though, when the relief officer, who read of the awards in the newspaper, accused him of concealing his eight-dollar prize money (which he hadn't yet received) and ordered him to work at the Woodlawn Cemetery for a few days until he made up the sum in labor.

Hurley exhibited at the local fair for the next three years, winning a first in 1935, a first and a second in 1936, and a second in 1937. Edith Tyrie, whose father had operated the first framing and art-supply business in Saskatoon and had handled Kenderdine's paintings, was for many years a judge of the pictures at the Exhibition and also kept watch over the art display during Exhibition week. She recalls that the art displays of the 1930's were usually large and fairly representative of the work being done in Saskatoon and in smaller centers, for it provided the one opportunity for artists to have their work exhibited. Small shows were occasionally mounted in store windows, but the Exhibition display was the showcase for art in Saskatoon. Not only did the displays attract many entries, she says, but they also attracted thousands of spectators, and she gives much of the credit for their success to the enthusiasm and interest of the Exhibition's manager, Sid Johns, generally referred to as "Mr. Showman" because of his flair for staging "bigger and better" fairs each year.

From Saskatoon, a great many of the pictures went to the Regina Exhibition. Norman Mackenzie, a lawyer and art collector in Saskatchewan's capital — the Norman Mackenzie Art Gallery, which houses his collection, was built with money left by him — would come to Saskatoon to select the entries for the Regina show; so the artists received wider-than-local recognition.

In 1934, the Hurleys moved from Victoria Avenue to the northern limits of the city at 1319 First Avenue North, near the Robin Hood Mill, where most of the people in the neighborhood were, like them, on relief. Their next-door neighbor was Horace Parker, who was one of the many amateur painters around Saskatoon at that time. It was after he became friendly with Mr. Parker that Hurley began to think seriously about art. The two enjoyed each other's company, shared such chores around their yard as wood cutting and stacking, held long and questioning conversations about art and life and what have you, and made countless sketching trips in the vicinity.

One of their favorite routes was north on the Warman road to old Factoria, a subdivision which had been touted in 1912 as "the magic city" with the promise of a million dollars' worth of industries and a population of 2,000 in its first year. All that was left of the dream of glory in 1934 were a few dilapidated buildings and the power booster station which was to serve the industrial area. In 1972, sixty years after Factoria was advertised as "the magic city," the site would stun those who had visualized it as the industrial mecca of the prairie town, for one of the city's finest residential areas has extended to its very doorstep.

The mid-thirties stand out in the story of Mr. Hurley's development as an artist as a time of great excitement. Not only did he meet Horace Parker, but at Lindner's he met others with whom he was to enjoy close and valued associations for many years, as, for instance, Dr. L. G. "Les" Saunders and Mashel Teitelbaum. With some of them he attended evening sketching sessions at the Tyrie art-framing studio, where they sketched from live models. Among those whom he met at the sketching class and who became lifelong friends were Stanley Brunst and H. W. Wickenden. The sketching class was valuable for Hurley, too, because of the free exchange of criticism among the artists and for the training it provided in draftsmanship. He had always enjoyed drawing from the time in England when he discovered that the problems of perspective held no mystery for him — his letters home were filled with drawings of his activities; now he applied himself seriously. It was impossible to sketch outdoors during the Saskatchewan winters; the class, among like-minded companions, was a bracing and challenging experience.

A man out of work is a man with time on his hands, but Bob Hurley

filled the time with sketching and painting. He sketched objects around the house, and he used pictures in books as sources of inspiration. And always he kept working at improving his water-color technique, referring, when he felt the need for help, to the book by Richmond and Littlejohns. Lack of proper equipment and materials led him to begin experimenting with what he had on hand. He tried laying on washes with discarded and ragged brushes that had been used for painting shelves and furniture, and found that he got some quite unusual effects; he retrieved toothbrushes that could no longer get teeth clean, and used them to spatter color through stencils. Because he had to call on all his power of invention, he found his experiments stimulating and "great good fun."

Most of his early paintings were done on paper cuttings left over from orders supplied to their customers by Hazen-Twiss, a book, stationery, and art-supply store on 22nd Street at Third Avenue. The off-cuts were generally small, and he used a flour paste to prepare the paper for painting. In a year or so he had enough paintings accumulated to set up a display in the Hazen-Twiss windows. A young, rosy-cheeked Englishman, more often taken for a student than for the professor of chemistry that he was, purchased a study of wild roses from that display. The support and encouragement of Dr. J. W. T. Spinks, now president of the University of Saskatchewan, continued over the years.

In a press report of the Hazen-Twiss display, the reporter referred to Hurley's method of spraying pigments with a toothbrush. In his first experiments with brushes of all kinds on papers of all sorts, using colors extracted from such sources as beets, vegetable greens, and tea, Hurley had the pleasure and the inspiration of the company of Stan Brunst. Almost from the moment of their meeting, Hurley and Brunst proved to be the most compatible of companions, and their close association during the remainder of the 1930's, until Brunst went to the West Coast, was a cherished one for Hurley. They continued their friendship by correspondence until Brunst's tragic death in a car crash in 1958. "The best friend I ever had," wrote Hurley at that time, in sadness.

The two men had much in common. Brunst, like Hurley, was born in 1894 in England. He was educated in the Royal Orphanage, Wolverhampton, but his schooling ended at the equivalent of grade seven. He emigrated to Canada in 1923 and worked on Saskatchewan farms before settling in Saskatoon where he was employed in a dry-cleaning plant. He did his first original work in water color in 1931. Brunst had a great facility for invention, and the two spent whatever hours Brunst could find, sketching, devising new techniques, and criticizing each other's ideas and efforts.

Brunst and Hurley went, by foot, on scores of sketching expeditions,

Hurley's sketch of the booster barn, one of the few buildings remaining at Factoria in 1934, with color notes added for future references

pencil

their favorite grounds being the river bank stretching east and north from the C.P.R. Bridge at 33rd Street. This area was popularly known as Goldeye Bay, but the two friends called it "The Magic Mile" (Plate IX). Like Factoria, The Magic Mile is now within the built-up area of the city, but long after Brunst had left, Hurley would wander along the bank, sketching and remembering their good times together.

Brunst poured over the art books in the Public Library and delighted in painting pictures after the fashion of other artists — à la Picasso, à la Braque, and so on. In his original work, he tended increasingly toward the abstract, and in Vancouver, he had a two-man show with the acknowledged master of the abstract in Canada at that time, Lawren Harris. His influence on Hurley was great. Not from a technical point of view, but as a source of inspiration and encouragement. After he went away he continued to send accounts of his experiments with different techniques: in 1950, for instance, he sent Hurley some dye pencils for Christmas, with a long letter about how to use them in water-color painting (Hurley didn't take to them, perhaps because Brunst wasn't around to prod him); and in 1954, for Bob's birthday, he sent some etchings, reporting that he found scrap sheet metal from a tinsmith shop a good and cheap substitute for copper plate.

It was Brunst who introduced Hurley to the enjoyment of listening to classical music, and listening to such music quickly became, and has remained, Hurley's chief delight. There were many times when he was too tired to paint or to read, and during those hours, in addition to prayer, he found solace and inspiration in music. Shortly after his interest in music was aroused, it received a tremendous boost when Mashel Teitelbaum, the young student and artist he had met at Lindner's, introduced him to Neil Chotem — Mashel painted an oil portrait of Hurley leaning against the grand piano in Neil's studio, but Hurley doesn't know what has become of the painting. Neil Chotem, who had been a child protégé in Saskatoon, introduced Hurley to his teacher, Lyell Gustin.

A few years later, Mr. Hurley had the exquisite pleasure of attending one of the combined art and music programs at the Gustin studio, a program which featured the water colors of Robert Hurley and the kind of music that the artist loved, played by Mr. Gustin's accomplished students. "His choice of music," Mr. Gustin recalls, "was the clear classical style of Mozart, the tonal warmth of Chopin and the pastel shading of Debussy."

It was the encouragement he received during the depression years from patrons like Mr. Gustin, Dr. Spinks, and Mr. Wood that gave him the will and determination, Hurley says, to keep on with his painting and to strive for improvement.

So familiar did Hurley become with the works of the composers he admired that he heard their music even when it was not being played. He loved to play selections from the classics on his guitar or harmonicas (he had seven of them), adapting them by changing certain octaves. And he began the practice of singing his favorite hymns and psalms to different classical airs, one of his favored sources being Mozart's "Don Giovanni." He has dozens of tunes for each hymn, ranging through Mozart, Bach, Vivaldi, Chopin, Boccherini, Handel, to Sibelius.

Naturally, he considered the radio as one of God's wonderful gifts to man when he heard music that he liked. CBC Wednesday Nights were a chosen listening time for him, as were the New York Philharmonic hours on Sundays. One Wednesday night, for instance, when he was painting in the kitchen, he "heard a very unusual work by the composer Cimarosa. It was his concerto for oboe and strings which I mistook for an unknown Mozart. A very lovely piece of music." A few days later, he heard a "tripe song" on his radio, and remarked that there "should be a law making such stuff a punishable offence." He had come a long way in music appreciation from the boy who had attempted to write a catchy song in order to win his way to fame and fortune.

In 1965, after the Beatles, in his words "crumby looking clowns," had been included in the Honors list of the Queen, he referred to them as "manufacturers of cacophony," and to their music as "distortions of the melodic line." Mr. Hurley has always been as vehement in his dislikes as in his likes. However, when asked, in 1972, if he had changed his mind about the Beatles, he readily admitted that he hadn't really paid much attention to them — he had just been shocked that such a group had been singled out for Royal approval. He doesn't reserve his dislike for popular music only; as one would expect, he doesn't like the music of Wagner, and he is repelled by the "bombastic, noisy 'Graduation' music by Strauss." He likes the music from many operas, but can't often endure "two hours or so of screeching in a foreign language."

For Hurley, as for Sir Thomas Browne, "There is music wherever there is harmony, order, or proportion; and thus far we may maintain the music of the spheres."

Harmony, order, proportion — those were the qualities Mr. Hurley was striving after in his paintings. More and more he tended to eliminate inessentials, and to concentrate on patterns, rhythms, and shapes. In 1937, when a show in Miss Tyrie's studio included some Hurley water colors, a writer in the *Star-Phoenix* remarked on the "marked improvement" in Hurley's work which "shows strong individuality in treatment and is notable for clear, strong color. The clarity of western atmosphere is excellently interpreted."

In addition to gaining more and more attention locally, Hurley found a measure of recognition on the national scene. Paintings by Hurley and Brunst were hung in a Vancouver gallery in 1937 and 1939. In 1938, Hurley, Brunst, Lindner, and Fred Steiger, who had a studio in the same building as Miss Tyrie's, had paintings accepted by the Ontario Society of Artists, the generally accepted arbiter of worth on the national level, and they were accepted again in 1939 by the O.S.A. Also, their paintings were shown in Winnipeg at the exhibitions of the Manitoba Art Association. One of the paintings Hurley sent to Toronto, "Roof Tops," was reproduced in the *Star-Phoenix;* strangely enough it bore a resemblance to "House Tops in the Ward," a much earlier painting by A. J. Casson (reproduced in *Painting in Canada*), a Canadian artist Hurley particularly admires, but in 1938 he wasn't familiar with Casson's work — he hadn't even heard of the Group of Seven artist.

However, framing and mailing paintings for acceptance in shows across the country cost more money than Hurley could afford and he didn't pursue the glory of wide acclaim. In any event, by 1940, the time was not too far off when sending paintings away for the purpose of gaining recognition would seem like folly to an artist who couldn't keep pace with the demand for his paintings at home.

As early as 1933, Hurley had started making quick pencil sketches of particular cloud arrangements, sky effects, and atmospheric conditions, adding notes on colors. As Western Canadian skies change rapidly, the quick sketches were his surest way of capturing a unique quality in the landscape. When he hadn't time to stop and sketch, or when he found himself without pencil and paper, he trained his memory to retain a particular scene until he had an opportunity to get it on paper. From the sketches he would build up finished paintings at his leisure, and he discovered that by varying the relationship of the planes and altering the color schemes, he could produce several paintings from one sketch, each quite different in total effect from the others. Sketching paper was the one kind he seldom lacked in the thirties, as Mashel had found a free source of supply from Harley Brown, the head pressman at the *Star-Phoenix*. The ends of rolls of newsprint were of no use to the paper but were of great value to the sketchers.

Supplied with wads of newsprint and a pencil, he was ready to go on a sketching trip with anybody who suggested one. One of his most frequent companions was Mr. Wickenden, whom he came to know affectionately as "Wick," or "Wicky." Mr. Wickenden had asked Hurley for some advice about his garden, and their association blossomed into a sketching partnership that lasted many years. Their opinions on many subjects, including religion,

Hurley included the figure of Mr. Wickenden on one of their many sketching trips, and pasted with the sketch in his collection a photograph of "Wick" in a typical pose — rolling a cigarette and enjoying the outdoors.

pencil and India ink

didn't match, but their feeling about art and their love of the outdoors were mutual.

Occasionally Hurley would go sketching with a group, usually in Les Saunders' car, with Lindner, Ernest Smith, Tom Buckley, and Bill Compton completing the number. Yorath Island, which was reached by driving south along the west bank of the river for a few miles, provided tempting spots for sketching (Plate XVI). The group would scatter for several hours and then meet to gather wood for a fire, cook their supper, and enjoy music supplied by Lindner on his mandolin and Hurley on his guitar. The good fellowship of those days took much of the sting from poverty.

During the winter of 1938-39, a group of artists obtained permission to hold sketching sessions in the studio in the Physics Building which Kenderdine had occupied until his departure for Regina in 1936. When word spread around that they were going to have a nude model, so many "artists" flocked to the first session that the plans for the evening had to be changed. After that, it was pretty much a closed group that met behind closed doors. Although not a class in the strict sense of the word, it served the same purpose, for the members freely exchanged criticisms. It was the last "class" that Hurley attended. The next time he was associated with a class, he was the teacher: but that was some time away.

Hurley liked figure drawing, and often sketched Isabella at work or the children at play. Another pastime during winter months was to go to windows in the C.N.R. station and in Eaton's store and sketch the crowds scuttling along the streets below. (See end papers). He thinks he might have developed in the direction of figure painting if he hadn't discovered early that landscapes sold more readily.

Towards the end of the decade his water colors were becoming known enough that the news editor of the *Star-Phoenix,* passing him on Second Avenue pushing a broom, stopping to ask what he was doing, and being informed that he had to do street cleaning to pay his electric light bill, could remark, "It's a goddam shame!"

Mashel Teitelbaum, who had been watching Hurley's development since they had met in 1933, wrote about him in *The Sheaf,* the University of Saskatchewan students' paper, on October the twenty-fourth, 1939, and said, in part:

"Compositionally, he achieves wide variety, in some papers his compositions are held together by a unity of mass and color relationships; in others by the inner logic of rhythmical lines and well thought designs. In writing about Hurley one is tempted to run the full gamut of superlatives, for he is a genuine artist and little known. Yet superlatives would neither suit the man nor his work. His painting stems from an intense love of nature. He is a conscious seeker of truth and beauty . . . in nature he hopes to find manifestation of God."

Hurley liked figure drawing and often sketched Isabella at work and the children at play.

pencil

Mashel also quoted a Paris art critic, Gerome Duquesnay, who, in an article planned for publication in *La Revue Moderne,* said: " Hurley is a modern mind, a temperament open to development — self-taught — it is to this fact that he owes his originality and the independence of style — a style all his own ... simple and so devoid of artifice ... The work of this artist deserves a place apart among contemporary Canadian water-color painters."

High praise, especially for a man who still considered himself a novice as a water-colorist!

While Hurley was enjoying his adventures in painting and his new associations, he was not blind to his responsibilities. His friend Brunst had gone to the West Coast to work in 1940; his neighbor Horace Parker had found employment running a night sweeper in the city yards. Hurley had found nothing to do. He and Isabella had made good and loyal friends apart from the art circle, particularly Norman Caplin, a young student who usually shared their Sunday dinners with them. In return, he donated his worn-out clothing for Isabella to convert into suits for Chuck. As Isabella says, "The poor helped the poor." The Hurleys had had another child, Alice, in 1935, and by 1941 they were wondering if they would ever be able to give their children the home they wished for them.

In this mood, Bob, late in 1941, arranged with the relief office for money to go to the West Coast to look for work, as there was talk of moving the Japanese inland, leaving coastal jobs vacant for "non-aliens." While he was away, Mr. Wood, a man who had already given his support to Hurley and who knew the plight the family was in, arranged with Mrs. Hurley for a one-man show at the Public Library.

Even with the help of Brunst at the Coast, Hurley was not successful in finding employment — he was, after all, forty-seven and not robust. He returned, disappointed but not downcast, for he still had his faith that all would turn out well. And he returned to find that the one-man show arranged by Mr. Wood had been successful from the financial point of view to the tune of $125, and to read Mr. Wood's comment: "Hurley is a far greater artist than anyone now realizes."

7

On The Way

THE 1930'S WERE the formative years for Hurley as an artist. In addition to the encouragement he received through the sketching classes and trips, the shows, the write-ups, the recognition by many individuals, and through his own increasing confidence in the skill he was acquiring through long hours at his worktable, he was influenced, willy-nilly, by the temper of the times, not from the gloom of the depressed economic conditions but from a something that was in the air that was making people in all walks of life re-examine values and attitudes. In Western Canada its most vivid outward expression was through political agitation which resulted in the founding of the Co-operative Commonwealth Federation (the CCF) in 1933. Hurley — surprisingly, considering his background of poverty and unemployment — was not a political animal. He had never felt any urge to take part in protest meetings against anything or to involve himself in plans for social improvements. It was the subtle change in public sentiment about the desirability of providing everyone with at least the opportunity to lead a good life that was to have importance for Robert Hurley. In terms of art, the sentiment was summed up by Arthur Lismer in his definition of art education, as reported in a Regina newspaper in 1932 (quoted in *September Gale*):

"Real child art education aims not so much to create artists as to teach Canadian children to use their eyes, make them aware of the beauty of life around them, and illuminate with some rays of beauty the tremendous fund of material which life and education has given to them. Then they never lose this sense of creative beauty in the outlook upon life around them, whether they become artists, poets, musicians, or people in other callings who appreciate and are aware . . ."

Eric Brown, the director of the National Gallery, who had championed the new nationalism of the Group of Seven, had traveled across Canada in 1931 and had been impressed by evidences everywhere of growing interest in art, not particularly through the public's appreciation of pictures in frames but through their awareness of the beauties of their surroundings, and by the new growth of art movements and art associations. Brown had great faith in the value of public lecturing as a kindling power for art, and he arranged a Western Canadian tour for Arthur Lismer for the spring of 1932.

Lismer visited Winnipeg, Regina, Calgary, Vancouver, Victoria, Edmonton, Saskatoon, and Prince Albert. He delivered about forty major addresses to a total of between five and six thousand people, and he spoke far more than forty times to small groups and societies. He was enthusiastic about the reception he received in all cities and about the intense interest he found in art. His message to the people was that they should open their eyes to their surroundings, and to the artists, that they should interpret their surroundings in their individual ways. "The artist," he said in one of his speeches, "uses nature in its present aspect not as a standard to copy, but as a source of inspiration."

The age of regionalism had dawned.

Once it was accepted that the techniques of the past and those used to interpret other countries were not necessarily the ones which should be used to interpret Canada, the artists were free to develop their own methods and styles. In the 1930's this freedom led to regionalism in art, for the depression made it virtually impossible for the artists to travel and to study in the great centers, which at that time was the only form of communication, apart from books. The depression made people prisoners of their own localities. In many ways it was a morale-destroying time, especially for young people who were forced to give up educational plans and who were faced with the prospect of no money, no work, no hopes; in other ways, it was a time which forced people to depend on their own resources to make life bearable — and painting, for a number of persons, became one of those resources.

In Saskatoon — indeed, in Saskatchewan — the number of artists who practiced techniques learned in other places at other times could be counted on one hand. There is a tendency today to write off much of their work as being marred by their technical training and outlook brought from England, France, Holland, or even Ontario; but they were genuine artists nevertheless and the very fact that they stayed in Saskatchewan because they were attracted to the environment gave their best paintings an authenticity and validity which paintings by more transient artists have often lacked.

Kenderdine's paintings reflect his preference for prairie bluffs and woodlands. James Henderson, who was born and trained in Glasgow, arrived in Regina in 1910. He had intended only to visit the country, but he became enamored of the West, and after a few years in Regina where he was engaged in commercial work, he moved permanently to Qu'Appelle in 1916. He became noted for his paintings of the Indians on nearby reserves and for his landscapes of the valley in every season. Joseph Henry Lee-Grayson was born in Harrogate and trained in England, France, and Holland before coming to Canada in 1906, and to Regina in 1908. After service in World War I, he returned to Regina where he became an enthusiastic water-color painter of the prairie landscape. English-born Inglis Sheldon-Williams homesteaded at Cannington Manor southeast of Regina in the nineteenth century, returned to England to study at the Slade School, and came back to Canada in 1913 to teach for four years at Regina College. His influence on art in Regina continued long after his career as a teacher. Hilda Stewart, daughter of two well-known London artists, was trained at home, at the Royal Academy Schools, and at the Regent Street Polytechnic. She was best known for her miniatures and was elected to full membership in the Royal Society of Miniature Painters, Sculptors and Gravers in London in 1927. She came to Canada in 1921, and was appointed instructor in art at Regina College in 1934, following the death of her husband. In 1936 Mrs. Stewart changed places with Kenderdine and continued to live in Saskatoon until her retirement in 1948. These were the immigrant professional artists in Saskatchewan. They weren't much concerned with influencing others, with the exception of Sheldon-Williams.

Illingworth H. Kerr has the distinction of being the first native-born professional artist. He returned to Lumsden in the Qu'Appelle Valley after studying in Toronto at the Central Technical School and the Ontario College of Art. By 1931, according to write-ups in the *Regina Leader-Post,* he had become a well-established artist. By 1934 he was feeling the isolation of living in a region where there was no professional society and he had some correspondence with Lindner about the possibility of founding a Saskatchewan society to establish and maintain standards. He battled the depression by traveling across the south of the province as a sign painter and by running a trapline in the north, but it defeated him in 1937 and he took off for England on a cattle boat. The province lost one of its most creative spirits. When he finally returned to Canada, he went to Vancouver and then to Calgary.

Hurley, then, was an absolute amateur in very much an amateur setting. Lindner was concerned about establishing a professional reputation, as was Steiger, who worked rather as a lone wolf and who left Saskatoon after the outbreak of war to make his way as an artist in the East. There were young people interested in studying art, but there was no art school in the province and they had no money to study elsewhere. One of the fortunate ones was Charles Lemery who went to study in Chicago and San Francisco but was unable to find any opportunity to use his training and his talents when he returned to Saskatoon in the late 1930's and so left for the United States. Mashel Teitelbaum, the youngest of Hurley's associates in the sketching groups, was determined to become a serious artist and was to continue his studies later.

The amateur atmosphere was one which appealed to Hurley, who could have been easily discouraged by too much formidable professionalism. He felt himself to be among friends with similar interests. Horace Parker was, like him, on relief. Stanley Brunst had, like him, very little formal education. Ernest Lindner had an enthusiasm which spilled over on all his students to the point of making them aware of art even if they couldn't manage the technical problems. The good companionship of Wickenden overcame Hurley's awe of him as a teacher of English in a city high school.

Not only did the art atmosphere of the 1930's in Saskatoon suit Hurley, but it also shaped the way he would develop as an artist. Lismer's call to the artists of the West to depict their environment with a fresh vision was a call that made sense to the painters in Saskatchewan, especially those in Saskatoon where the influence of a Constable-inspired Sheldon-Williams had not affected the outlook of the amateurs as it had in Regina. Kenderdine possessed a highly independent and original personality, and he valued independence and originality in others. He encouraged his students to think and to see for themselves, for to Gus, the ability to express oneself was more important than the talent to copy another's style.

Nor did the Western painters live under the awesome shadow of the reputation of the Group of Seven as did those in the East. The personal influence of the members of the Group had extended as far west as Winnipeg, where Franz Johnston, one of the original members, was principal of the Winnipeg School of Art from 1920-24, and where L. L. Fitzgerald, one of the Group's later members, began teaching in 1929. Illingworth Kerr was the only Saskatchewan artist to have come directly under the influence of the Group when he studied at the Ontario College of Art during the years when J. E. H. MacDonald was the principal.

Not that the painters in Saskatoon were unaware of the significance of the Group in the development of painting in Canada. They were as excited and delighted as others about the achievement of the Group in freeing Canadian painting from academic and alien conventions. They were in the fortunate position of being able to enjoy the freedom which the Group had won without feeling overawed by the Group's influence. Exhibitions arranged by the National Gallery were hung at the University of Saskatchewan from time to time, which provided the Saskatoon artists with an opportunity to study Canadian originals. Lindner was strongly attracted by the work of Tom Thomson. Hurley, when he began to take notice of the work of other current artists, was drawn to the work of Casson.

"Art is not something superimposed from without and from another age, but it is an interpretation of contemporary life. . . . Art is something within an artist responding to the call of life and beauty. A love of one's own environment is requisite." So Lismer was reported in Regina. In Edmonton, the report went: " 'Amateur artists will never get anywhere except with amateur minds,' declared Mr. Lismer, explaining the dangers of imitation and rigid adherence to technique. 'People want to know what they have to say in their own way and not in other people's ways.' "

For Hurley, the freedom to paint the environment in his own way had a deep significance, for to him, nature and the human form were the works of God. Through his paintings he was able to praise the Great Designer.

From October to December, 1938, Mr. Hurley kept a diary, his first attempt at writing down his thoughts and observations. He refers frequently to the idea of a Great Designer. By that time he had been attracted to British-Israelism and to the science of numerology as expounded by such writers as Rudolph Steiner and Rom Landau.

"Working in the back garden today," he wrote, "I am reminded of the tremendous profusion of nature manifested in a sunflower head, which measured fourteen inches in diameter. To count the number of seeds the circumference was traced and the resulting diagram ruled in one-inch square sections. Twenty-five seeds to the inch square was the average count, totaling 3,000 seeds for the complete head. . . . The numerical order of the humble sunflower is matched with the geometrical design of the seed arrangement, the 3,000 seeds tracing an intricate overlapping design. . . .

"The sunflower pollen has the ray-like character of the gay whole head, when viewed under a microscope, and the gray-black seeds are triangular. . . .

"Sometime I would like to study seeds under the microscope and paint the enlarged forms in water color. I am sure it would be a fascinating hobby.

"I am forced," he continued, "to think of the Great Designer, and see a simple mathematical order in nature's handiwork, this same numerical structure interlocks with the Scriptures. . . . Of course the evolutionist, rationalist and mechanist, all differ and propound conflicting theories.

"St. John's Gospel states, Chapter IV: 3, 'All things were made by Him; and without Him was not anything made that was made.' Shall we accept Darwin, agree with Ingersoll, Kant and Paine, or believe God's explanation of the creation of living things?"

He was fascinated by the "infinite variety of design in the snow crystal," with a fundamental structure of six or three. "Fifty years ago," he commented, "Sir John Herschel proposed the value of the Pyramid inch to be the true earth commensurate unit. Is it all a purposeless chaos, or is a benevolent being revealing his majesty?"

After describing the colors, shadows, and shapes in a few feet of snow along the fence, he remarked: "These treasures of a colorful winter landscape are unobserved by the majority, reminding one of the eternal treasures of the Bible, likewise unknown to the masses."

He was reading Jean Henri Fabre's *The Life of the Spider* and *The Marvels of the Insect World,* and queried: "Fabre has much interesting information about these Arachnidae. . . . Did these forty families evolve 100,000,000 years ago from primordial slime or is there a Great Designer?"

The writings of John James Audubon and of William Beebe were also among his favorite studies. Beebe's account of a marine creature that possessed a built-in luminous device brought forth this comment: "Down in the realms of perpetual night we have an outstanding witness of the Wise Creator in the bestowal of luminosity to illumine gloom."

Naturalist on the Amazon by Henry W. Bates fascinated Hurley for years. In 1951 he was reading it for the fourth time and deriving as much pleasure from it as he had on his first reading. Indeed, his armchair trips to faraway lands became sort of sketching expeditions. Many of his paintings which depict fish and birds and insects were based on his reading experiences. In his linocut designs of the 1930's, his knowledge of exotic fish and birds often supplied his inspiration. And perhaps he had retained memories of the goldfish he liked to watch as a little boy at the home of his friend, Harry Fiveash, and of the tropical birds in the London zoo.

He found inspiration wherever he looked. "My basement today revealed design and rhythm in ever-changing variety in the marking of the wall timber," he wrote. "I drew over twenty different designs from the curious grainings in the boards, each one adaptable for fabric design." And outside his back door that same day he stopped to examine the seven-figured footprints left by a dog. "Yet," he commented, "these wonderful facts escape the notice of humanity in its frantic struggle for pleasure, wealth or prestige."

"The Great Architect and Designer of the Universe has set around us all an inexhaustible storehouse of loveliness and order, so why waste good paint and canvas on the disgustingly freakish or chaotic?" he wrote in a letter protesting against "modern" painting, published in the *Star-Phoenix* in 1955.

Even as Mr. Hurley saw all nature as the creation of a Great Designer, so he saw nature as reflecting the Creator.

"The horizontal cloud formations suggest rest and peace, like a vast benevolent hand outstretched in blessing and tenderness, bidding man to cease from labor. I definitely sense that Divine sweet brooding overshadowing any landscape. . . ."

There were times, too, when he sensed nature to be a participant in events:

"There is a sense of rest and peace in all nature very noticeable on the Sabbath Day. . . . The weather on Good Friday is usually in keeping with the tragic, awful event."

8

At The Lab

ON GOOD FRIDAY, 1942, Bob Hurley was preparing for a trip to the Scott Experimental Farm about sixty miles west of Saskatoon in the Unity-Wilkie district, where there was the prospect of a job, when he was called by a neighbor to the telephone.

"Good news," a voice said. "It's all set."

The call was from Dr. P. M. Simmonds, head of the Dominion Plant Pathology Laboratory, a branch of the Canada Department of Agriculture Research Station, in Saskatoon. Hurley had met Dr. Simmonds some months before through Mr. Lindner, who occasionally drew some charts for the lab, and when he had first called at the laboratory with samples of his work, "P.M.," as the chief was generally known, had immediately bought a small landscape and had urged a co-worker, Dr. Ralph C. Russell, to buy a study of zinnias. Hurley had painted the landscape, "Birch Trees," on a sketching trip with Lindner and Saunders to the spot where Eagle Creek empties into the North Saskatchewan River, about forty miles west of Saskatoon near Borden. Sixteen years later, when Hurley retired from his laboratory work, Dr. Simmonds presented him with the little painting, which now hangs in the Hurley home in Victoria, a pleasant reminder of his good fortune on that memorable Good Friday and of his happy and rewarding years at the lab.

The job at the laboratory had become available when A. W. Davey, who later worked as an artist for the Government in Regina, had enlisted. Hurley's ability to draw and his gardening experience made him an eligible candidate, although for the most part the chores were to be of the caretaking kind. In March, Hurley had observed his forty-eighth birthday; there had been no cause for a celebration. The Hurleys had been on relief for eight and a half years!

At the beginning, he was employed on a temporary basis and paid thirty cents an hour. He usually was at work before nine in the morning and stayed until after five. With a few extra hours on Saturdays and Sundays, when he had to check on moisture and temperatures, he was able to earn as much as fifty dollars a month. In about a year, he had to pass a civil service examination in order to be retained on a semi-permanent basis; there were seventy multiple-choice questions, which terrified him. After the examination, Dr. Simmonds happened to be in his office one Saturday morning when Bob arrived to do his chores. "Come here for a minute,

Hurley sketching the reflections he so loved to paint

Hurley," he called, and taking his pipe from his mouth for four or five seconds, he announced, "Good news. You passed!" It was indeed good news, for it meant an increase in salary, cost-of-living bonus, and annual holidays of three weeks with pay.

The plant pathology laboratory was located in the greenhouses back of the College (now Administration) Building on the University of Saskatchewan campus. As it was three miles or so from the Hurleys' home near the Robin Hood Mill, Isabella decided it was time for a move. After investigating available accommodation in the university district, she settled for a house on Railway Avenue in Sutherland, a town connecting with the eastern limits of the campus. Bob, at first, wasn't enthusiastic about moving to Sutherland; he had become attached to his sketching country in the North Park district. They moved, and it wasn't too long before he admitted that Isabella had been right.

After a few months of renting the Railway Avenue house, the Hurleys purchased it for $750. Isabella was the handyman of the family — in the winter of 1943-44 she took a course in manual training at the Technical Collegiate — and with her polishing, painting, repairing, and sewing, she soon had the house turned into a comfortable home. She took an immediate liking to Sutherland, considering it an ideal place to bring up the two children. In 1942, Chuck was nine and Alice was seven.

There was an hourly bus service from Sutherland past the university, which would get Bob to work in a matter of minutes. On fine days, when he was feeling strong, he enjoyed walking. More often than not on the early morning and evening walks, even if they were just to and from the bus, he mentally recorded ideas for paintings, keeping the image in his mind until he had a chance to make one of his shorthand sketches.

"Memorized a landscape at 8:25 going to the bus. Wispy orange horizon, clouds with bright band of deep ultra overhead." "Dawn came with a heavy downfall of snow. Did a memory sketch of this wintry dawn. A gray-blue cloud curtain in the southeast. Pure white snow on roofs, buildings, and earth, some ochre-colored grass and sienna brush contrasting with the dazzling ice powder."

Best of all, Sutherland itself, which had retained the appearance of a prairie town, proved to be a goldmine for sketching (Plate XXI.) Railway tracks, telephone poles, grain elevators were his environment. In the spring, when the elevators were reflected in the sloughs, he could paint them practically from his doorstep. "Did four pencil sketches of buildings reflected in pools of snow water. I love doing these." "Glorious day. Wandered around Sutherland. Six pencil sketches of elevators reflected in water pools." "Made first outdoor sketching trip around Sutherland this spring [1951] Seven sketches of snow water lakes, and reflected buildings which always make for pictorial inspiration." "Went scouting for pictorial ideas armed with sketch book, pencils, and water boots. Sky spectacular. Elevators reflected in water. Altogether I put in an enjoyable afternoon." So he recorded his spring Sutherland sketching trips in his diary (Plates XXII, XXV).

He could paint the elevators in all kinds of weather without going outside, for from one front window he looked directly down the railway tracks at them. For fourteen years, this window framed a typical "Hurley." And looking east from the kitchen window, he painted many sunrises, tumbling cloud effects, snowscapes, and nocturnes, for there were no tall buildings or hills to block his view of the sky.

Hurley treasured the early morning hours. He would rise at six or earlier, coax the stove into a blaze, have a prayer period in the kitchen, using his chair as his altar — "But God honors this" — and then see what the morning had to offer in the way of pictorial delights. Seldom was he left without inspiration, from receiving ideas for Christmas card designs from the patterns of the snow in the backyard or of the frost on the windowpanes, to hints of new and unusual color combinations to be applied to old sketches. Only when the sky was totally obscured by gray clouds, which seldom happened on the Prairies, was he left without fresh ideas.

To make up for the loss of Goldeye Bay as a sketching area within walking distance of his home, he had Sutherland Beach, almost opposite from his "Magic Mile." He liked to hike to the beach, especially on lovely spring days or during Indian summer, and he would sit for hours sketching the sandbars and rocks. One hot day, when he was absorbed in his sketching, he heard a voice say, "Mad dogs and Englishmen!" He turned and saw a familiar figure putting his pipe back in his mouth, shaking his head at the eccentricities of artists, and moving on to collect more bugs in a small jar of water. Hurley also shook his head, and went on sketching.

Hurley's world, when he moved to Sutherland, was thus enlarged to include another stretch of the river which had been such an important feature of his environment from the time he had settled in Saskatoon. He missed his old sketching partner and neighbor, Horace Parker, but Mr. Parker soon moved to British Columbia to work in the Empress Hotel in Victoria. In any event, Hurley's sketching time was limited to Saturdays, Tuesday afternoons (usually his half-day off), and holidays. Through his work at the laboratory, however, he enjoyed some wonderful and extended sketching trips when he accompanied the scientists on their visits to the experimental stations at Indian Head, Swift Current, and Scott, and on their trips to inspect selected fields of grain.

On one trip, in the fall of 1942, at the invitation of Dr. J. B. Harrington of the university's field husbandry department, he visited the Petersmeyers who owned one of the large-scale farms on the Regina plains, about sixteen miles from Regina. Unfortunately for Hurley, it rained, and the wet gumbo soil made it impossible for him to get out to do much sketching. The trip, however, brought him new contacts, for the Petersmeyers bought some of the paintings he had taken down from Sutherland, and on his way home he was interviewed by Mildred Valley Thornton for the *Regina Leader-Post*, who commented on the growing recognition of Hurley as a painter of prairie scenes and on his unusual "spatterwork" (toothbrush) technique.

The laboratory itself supplied Hurley with an almost unlimited supply of design ideas based on the lab equipment — test tubes, funnels, beakers, graduates, and the still for making distilled water for the plants. The old still was a temperamental apparatus and many times had to be teased into working. Finally its tubes became so corroded with lime that it stopped producing altogether. When it had to be dismantled to make way for a new still, there was mingled joy and sorrow. Hurley wrote one of his "jingles" about the last moments in the existence of the familiar tormentor:

> *Who broke the Still,*
> *"I," said Eddie, "with ax I was ready."*
> *"Good," agreed Bob, "Do a good job."*
> *"It's sure had its day," chortled Dr. B.J.*
> *Joined in the bustle was Dr. Ralph Russell.*
> *Even H. Mead, with this, well agreed.*
> *"But," wailed the Chief, "this gives me much grief."*
> *And Dr. Stan Chinn complained of the din,*
> *While Gladys, our steno, took notes with her pen-o,*
> *And Hurley, with glee-o, brewed up the tea-o.*

The atmosphere in the laboratory was one of informal friendliness, conducive to easing the tension involved in work that was necessarily of an exacting and patience-trying nature. In addition to the meticulous care which the experiments demanded, there was the fear of low temperatures damaging the seedlings — it didn't have to be winter, for Hurley noted in his diary at the end of April, 1956, that they had lost all plants in the protected cold frames; the worry about damage from a flooded basement in the spring, and the constant battle against mice. Even Dr. Simmonds' cat with the award-winning name of Oscar couldn't cope with the mice. On more than one occasion Hurley had to go to the university cafeteria for bacon rind bait because the mice were "Salading off Dr. Russell's barley seedlings."

The following is Hurley's description of a specimen workday: "Six A.M. wake up, light fire in kitchen, have prayer session. Throw up window

DR. BOB TINUNE · 1954.

R·N·HURLEY

shade. Do a pencil sketch of a colorful sunrise through east window. Catch city bus at 8:30 A.M. Arrive at university 8:45. Unlock labs, offices. Check steam and lights in greenhouses, labs. Unlock storeroom, glass room. 9:15 empty and burn waste paper. 10 A.M. go for mail. 10:15 get cup of coffee. 10:30 - 12 wash glassware, flasks, beakers. 12 noon to 1:30 eat lunch in lab, read or sleep. 1:30 count and cull barley or wheat kernels for a planting. 3 to 4 P.M. prepare soil and sand for sowing culled barley in. 4, afternoon coffee. 4:15 phone call from someone wanting a water color. 5:15 sweep through labs and fix things safe for the night. 5:45 catch bus for home."

It wasn't all work though, for there were days when things at the lab were slack, giving Hurley time for sketching or painting. In addition to writing jingles, he liked to amuse himself while waiting for a painting to dry by putting water at different levels in glasses of various shapes and sizes and playing a tune on them with some metal ribs he had retrieved from a worn-out corset. He built up quite a repertoire.

"It's very cozy working around the lab these cold days," he wrote one February, "but specially so in the greenhouse where the sun's light brings out the vivid shades of wheat and barley experiments."

Sometimes when Hurley was brewing the coffee and putting out the biscuits for the morning or afternoon break, he would think back to the days when he had worked in the London printing shop and had fetched the beer and tea for the men. The trips with the long rod holding the mugs seemed to him to have belonged not only to another time but to have happened to another person than the man who enjoyed the camaraderie in the lab. When he passed the hat for donations to the coffee fund, he was grateful that he could contribute his share, sometimes more than his share, for he liked buying some goodies in the way of a treat now and then.

"Besides being lab technician, coffee brewer, mail distributor, greenhouse-man, and general factotum, I fill in as an artist," he wrote in the 1950's, noting that he was painting a map on linen for Dr. R. D. Tinline showing areas in North America invaded with rust spore coming up the valley of the Mississippi into Manitoba and Saskatchewan. Probably unknown to his subject, Hurley was also sketching Dr. Tinline, at his microscope. Dr. Tinline became head of the laboratory in 1962 when Dr. Simmonds retired, a short time before the Hurleys left Saskatoon to live in Victoria.

The men in the plant pathology laboratory — P. M. Simmonds, R. C. Russell, B. J. Sallans, R. D. Tinline, R. J. Ledingham, S. H. F. Chinn, and H. W. Mead — worked in close co-operation with the scientists in the other branches of the Canada Agriculture Research Station on the campus and with the faculties of a number of related university departments. Visitors

◄ *Dr. Bob Tinline, of the Canada Department of Agriculture Research Station*
blue ink

were numerous in the cozy greenhouses, and P.M.S. was always pleased when they showed an interest in the work of his lab assistant, frequently drawing their attention to Hurley's paintings like a proud father displaying the work of a gifted son. When distinguished scientists from other parts of Canada and from other countries were expected as visitors, Hurley would work like a beaver cleaning the labs to have everything in shipshape condition. Sometimes he would listen in on erudite and technical discussions and be amazed at the knowledge the learned men carried around in their heads; at other times he would be equally amazed at the commonplaces they exchanged. Once, when he was expecting a more than usually brilliant discussion, he listened in on a conversation which consisted mainly in comparing the merits of various cold-curing concoctions, with the noted visitor praising the relief to be had from drinking hot water flavored with lemon juice and laced with two ounces of gin.

"I get a big thrill meeting so many with degrees," Hurley had written in his diary a few days before, "Because I never went beyond grade six at Plasket Road London County School." Scientists, in his opinion, certainly did some unexpected things, even though the common cold was admittedly a subject of universal interest. The following Christmas when he had a chest cold and there was some brandy in the house — the first time the Hurleys had had any liquor in their home — he tried the hot water-lemon juice-alcohol concoction. He discovered that while it brought some temporary relief, it was no cure.

It would not be far-fetched to see the lab as the nursery of Robert Hurley's success as an artist, for it served as an ideal showcase for his paintings and it provided him with an ever-widening market for his work.

In 1942, the University of Saskatchewan was a small institution, very small in comparison to its size in 1972. The greenhouses could be reached in a ten-minute walk from any point on the wind-swept campus. College Building was only a stone's throw away from the laboratory where Hurley held sway with his broom and his brushes, and at some time or another during each year, everyone associated with the university had occasion to call in at that building as it housed the president, the registrar, the bursar, two or three deans, the library, and the bookstore — if only for the dire reason of being called up on the carpet for not having conformed to university regulations.

Unlike many artists who have to work hard to gain recognition by entering their work in competitions and arranging exhibitions in galleries, Robert Hurley had displays planned for him. All he had to do was to produce enough paintings. Mr. Wood had started the practice when he had arranged the successful one-man show in the library in 1941. In 1942 a permanent display of Hurley paintings was mounted in the university bookstore, with fresh pictures added from time to time as the ones on display were sold. The bookstore display led interested spectators to the Hurley hangout to see what else the artist might have for sale. The demand for Hurley paintings was not so great during World War II years that it taxed the artist's ability to meet it, but after the war the demand became as phenomenal as the growth of the university.

By 1944, however, when Robert Ayre, a Montreal art critic and an editor of *Canadian Art,* visited Saskatoon, he reported in an article on Hurley that the artist had sold more than fifty water colors to prominent citizens since 1942 and that four paintings were owned by the Public Library. The sale of fifty paintings in two years was a trickle compared with later sales, but it was a not inconsiderable number.

To receive the best and fullest impression of Mr. Hurley's paintings, Mr. Ayre wrote, it was desirable to see a dozen or twenty at a time, for they had a "cumulative effect" on the viewer, each adding to the enjoyment of the others.

In summing up his response to Hurley's achievement, Mr. Ayre said: "In his sense of space, in his contemplative calm, in the delicacy and economy of his handling, though he has no mountains, he reminds me of the Chinese . . . . Robert Hurley gives it (the prairie) to us in its undramatic, almost featureless, subtlety."

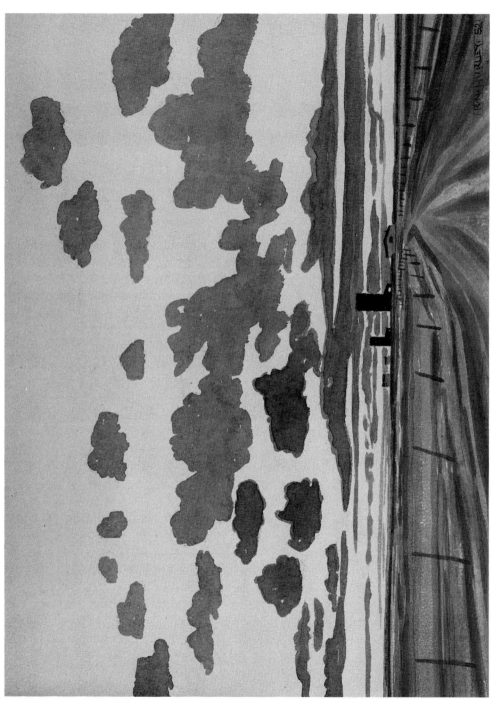

Evening 1952. 13¼ x 9¾''

9

An Aroused Public

WHEN DR. GORDON W. SNELGROVE opened the spring exhibition of the Saskatoon Art Association in 1942, he remarked that "our artists are opening our eyes every day to new beauties in our countryside," and he reminded his audience that Arthur Lismer, when he had opened the exhibition the previous spring during another cross-Canada tour, had stressed the need for local artists to paint purely local scenery.

One-half of the message which Lismer had preached to the public in his Western tour of 1932 — the need for artists to paint their local environment — was still in the air in the early 1940's. It was soon to be displaced, however, by a new nationalism which developed with the growing stature of Canada as a power during World War II, and which increased rapidly after the war when easy communication between parts of the country was established. Travel had been limited during the depression years, and restricted during the war. After the war, travel was not only not restricted, but with the airplane coming into its own, travel, even from one coast to the other, was speedier than most had dreamed possible. As the speed of communications increased, and as the new medium of television developed, nationalism was joined by internationalism. Instant communication, as Marshall McLuhan has said, makes the world a global village.

The Canadian artists who heralded the new isms had to battle public opinion, just as the Group of Seven had had to fight in the 1920's. Mr. Hurley was not one of them; rather, he tended to join with the public in expressing disapproval. When he attended a lecture by Dr. Snelgrove, head of the university's art department from 1936 until his death in 1966, on a traveling exhibition of Canadian paintings, in 1952, he lamented the fact that very few of the pictures showed the Canadian landscape. He called them "monstrosities on canvas."

Even if Hurley had wanted to break fresh ground in his art — and there are many indications in his diaries that he was tired of painting elevators and telephone poles — his admiring public gave him little opportunity. They wanted their typical "Hurleys" to such an extent that he was often unable physically to keep up with the demand.

The other half of Lismer's 1932 message — the need to arouse public interest — had not had much impact in Saskatchewan during the 1930's when the public looked at its battered environment with a justifiably jaundiced eye. Hurley had gained some recognition through stories in the press and through the efforts of Mr. Wood, but he had not sold many pictures. Very few people had money to spend on paintings. Art was a frill, not a necessity, and even an interest in art was shoved aside by more practical concerns, except for painters like Hurley, for whom art had a therapeutic value.

However, while scientists at the University of Saskatchewan and at the experimental stations fought to combat drought conditions and to develop improved grains, the university led the way in paying attention to the cultural needs of the distressed population.

In 1931 a chair of music was established through a gift from the Carnegie Corporation, and Arthur Collingwood was appointed dean of music. His students were few, but he enriched the musical life of the university and the city by founding the Saskatoon Symphony orchestra and by holding open-house record concerts in the theater of the Physics Building, which Mr. Hurley often attended. In 1936 a department of art was formally established when Dr. Snelgrove was appointed professor of art. In the same year a School of Fine Art was opened at Regina College through a bequest from Norman Mackenzie. Also, in 1936, the university acquired thirteen acres at Emma Lake, north of Prince Albert, and equipped it as an art camp.

Dr. Snelgrove lectured on art appreciation and on the history of art. Through the university's extension services, he traveled extensively throughout the province, giving dozens of lecture demonstrations. This indefatigable traveler was in much demand as a lecturer, and he contributed a great deal in arousing public interest in the visual arts. His night classes were always filled to capacity, attracting members of the public as well as students, some traveling for a hundred miles and more every week. As the thirties turned into the forties, a dint was being made in the public's apathy to art, although there was still a long way to go to the break-through. The next decade, however, was to be characterized by significant developments.

The 1940's were a time of organizational ferment, the organizations being designed to provide the artists with a united voice to promote their common aims, and to break through public indifference. In 1941, the Federation of Canadian Artists was formed following a meeting at Queen's University in Kingston, Ontario, sponsored by the National Gallery. Its purpose was to act as a collective spokesman for artists, and on occasion, to present briefs to appropriate bodies. Ernest Lindner was the Saskatchewan representative. In 1944, he was elected to the national executive, and it was through his urging that the Saskatoon Art Association became the Northern Saskatchewan Branch of the Federation of Canadian Artists, thus aligning itself with the spirit of nationalism that was sweeping the country.

The arrival of the Mendel family as refugees from Nazi Germany was a shot in the arm for art in Saskatchewan. Mr. Fred Mendel, who established the firm of Intercontinental Packers in Saskatoon, managed to bring with him the nucleus of his notable art collection, and his generous hospitality enabled many to see originals by famous modern European artists. He invited the members of the Saskatoon Art Association to visit his suite above his meat-packing plant one Sunday afternoon in late 1942, and arranged for their transportation by horse-drawn sleigh. Hurley was among the group, and had his first look at works by such masters as Franz Marc and Lyonel Feininger. He was attracted by the colors and the rhythmic movement in the Marc painting, but not by the subject matter — pigs. Hurley has never departed from his belief that the subject of a painting should have some connection with beauty, and while he apparently found cows acceptable, pigs were beyond the pale.

Mr. Mendel encouraged Saskatoon artists by attending local shows and selecting paintings for his collection. His artist-daughter Eva was a member of the Art Association. When she and Dr. Max Miller were married one of their wedding presents was a painting by Hurley from Hurley. The continuing interest of the Mendels in art, and their support of art in the city of their adoption, culminated in 1961 with Mr. Mendel's gift to Saskatoon of $175,000 for the building of an art gallery and his later donation to the gallery which bears his name of his collection of Canadian paintings, exclusive of local works.

The establishment of a permanent gallery — the Mendel Art Gallery was opened in the fall of 1964 — was the realization of a dream that took shape in the early 1940's when the members of the Art Association became increasingly frustrated by the need to rent temporary accommodation in order to hang the spring and fall exhibitions and by their inability to sponsor shows from other parts of Canada. The artists suffered from a feeling of isolation by not being able to see the work being done elsewhere except for the occasional National Gallery show hung at the university.

Together with the Camera Club and the Archeological Society, and aided by a small grant from the city council on the recommendation of Mayor A. W. Macpherson, the Art Association formed the Saskatoon Art Centre. Situated on the second floor of the Standard Trust Building on Third Avenue, across the street from Hazen-Twiss, the Art Centre was formally opened in May, 1944. Its creation was a bold move, but its success over the years, in spite of one rough period, justified it as an act of faith.

During its first six months of operation, more than 400 persons joined as members and more than 4,000 visited the twelve exhibitions that were hung. Exhibitions were sent to interested rural communities and were received with interest. The Art Centre also joined the Western Art Circuit, which had been formed about the same time under the sponsorship of the Federation of Canadian Artists, and brought in exhibitions from neighboring provinces. The Centre was run by a board of directors representing the three societies and was staffed by a part-time secretary. The work of hanging and taking down exhibitions was done by the enthusiastic artists, Hurley often helping and often with Isabella by his side.

One of the twelve exhibitions, on display for three weeks in August, was a two-man show featuring the works of Hurley and Hilda Stewart. What interested the *Star-Phoenix* reporter was the marked contrast between the styles of the two artists. Hurley's paintings, the report said, were attractive because of their clarity and simplicity; Mrs. Stewart's were attractive because of their delicacy and attention to detail. Both painted the Saskatchewan country, but each saw entirely different aspects of it. Hurley's paintings reflected his response to the drama of the skies and the starkness of prairie architecture, which he symbolized in the grain elevator; Mrs. Stewart's reflected her training in England and her skill as a miniaturist in her choice of gentle, almost pretty, subjects. Hurley's work was the more original, the more startling; Mrs. Stewart's the more finished and professional.

The Hurley-Stewart show attracted hundreds of visitors, including Dr. Max Stern, owner of the Dominion Gallery of Fine Art in Montreal. An unusual footnote to Dr. Stern's interest in Hurley paintings developed from his purchase of twenty water colors in 1951 to include in a showing of Western Canadian artists at the Dominion Gallery. Either at that time, or later, Lord Beaverbrook was at the Dominion Gallery and purchased a Hurley for his gallery in Fredericton, New Brunswick. Hurley heard of Lord Beaverbrook's possession of one of his paintings from Dr. C. Farstad, of the Lethbridge Experimental Station, who had seen it when visiting in Fredericton. It was after Mr. Hurley told Stanley Obodiac of this incident that Stanley, who was writing a book on Hurley (Mr. Obodiac was living in Yorkton at that time), dug up the information that it had been Beaverbrook's money that had brought Bob to Canada in 1923. Dr. Stern doesn't remember selling the picture to Beaverbrook, and it was, for some reason or other, later returned to Montreal, but "the Beaverbrook incident" remains a human-interest incident in Hurley's life, one of the many coincidences which he has found so miraculous.

In late November, 1944, Lawren Harris, president of the Federation of Canadian Artists, visited Regina and Saskatoon to discuss with civic and government officials the Federation's brief to the House of Commons Reconstruction Committee on the plan for community centers. Supported by the National Gallery, the Federation was proposing the construction of centers for the arts in large and small communities, not only to provide work for returning servicemen but also to help to improve living conditions.

There were lively discussions about the role of art in society. Hon. John H. Sturdy, Minister of Reconstruction and Rehabilitation in the Saskatchewan CCF Government, elected in June, said: "Certainly this Government is impressed with the importance of well established community centres in any postwar reconstruction programme. This Department, while only in the process of being organized, has already given consideration to the organization of community centres and will no doubt propose to the Federal Government their development on a share-cost basis."

Hon. W. S. Lloyd, Minister of Education, writing on the place of art in the school curriculum, said: "Art has long been a vital and essential factor in the life of man. The ability to create beauty adds much to the happiness and richness of life. Now, more than ever, the cultured individual desires beauty in his surroundings. In the elementary school our fundamental purpose is to train the child to see and appreciate the beauty in his environment, to give him experience in using various media to make beautiful things, and to enable him to apply art to his daily life as an individual and as a member of the social group. Art can in this way supply those enriching experiences which, like music, bind people of many races together in a common pursuit of worthwhile goals, and at the same time build in a very real sense the foundation of Canadian unity."

Mr. Lloyd went on to outline some of the changes which would be proposed in a revision of the high school curriculum. These included the recommendations that art become a regular subject in the course of studies carrying credit for university entrance, and that the university be asked to institute an art department which would be capable of preparing instructors in art both from the viewpoint of acquiring content and of learning methods of teaching.

And Watson Thomson, director of adult education in the Department of Education, expressed his opinion: "First, I believe that the condition of art in a country is the same question as that of the health of the social organism as a whole. Only when a people are 'on the march' does art find a healthy social function for itself. Maybe the people of Saskatchewan are now just beginning to acquire that general momentum and maybe, therefore, art in this province is about due for a rebirth. The social ferment of the post-war period, with the returned men playing an important part, may be a further stimulus in this direction.

"The other sort of stimulus should be by bringing to the people of this province other examples of great art. We hope to play a part in this aspect of the problem, in co-operation with the National Gallery people and their plans for regional art galleries." (Extracts from letters to the author, November, 1944.)

Canadians who were involved and interested in the arts in the mid-1940's were certainly "on the march." In 1945 the Canadian Arts Council was formed, with a membership of nineteen national societies, including the Federation of Canadian Artists. Mr. Lindner was the Saskatchewan representative at the founding meeting, and in 1947 he was elected a Western vice-president with instructions to press for the formation of a provincial body, a plan which the Saskatchewan Government had already in mind. With himself and Emrys Jones, professor of drama at the University of Saskatchewan, as citizen members of a planning committee, and David Smith and Sam Roddan of the adult education division of the Department of Education as Government representatives, the Saskatchewan Arts Board was designed, and it was established by order in council in 1947, with the first meeting held February the seventh, 1948.

In May, 1946, the first Provincial Art Exhibition was held at the Saskatoon Art Centre, organized and set up by the artist members. It was quite an undertaking, and some of the artists were feeling the strain of giving up hours of their time to help to promote art. With the formation of the Saskatchewan Arts Board, the provincial exhibitions later became its responsibility and they were opened in alternate years in Regina and Saskatoon. H. G. Glyde, of the University of Alberta's art department, was the judge of the 1946 show, the first jury show held, and he selected works by forty-six artists. Among the forty-six were Mr. Hurley and a newcomer to the art scene, Bill Perehudoff, a young farmer from the Langham district who had had a two-man show at the centre with Mashel Teitelbaum earlier that year.

The exhibitions and activities at the centre aroused a great deal of public interest. Membership and attendance kept increasing to the point where the board of directors decided the time had come to employ a full-time curator to take the burden of work off the artists' shoulders. The financial statement, while not glowing, seemed to justify the decision, and George Swinton, an enthusiastic, Montreal-trained artist, was appointed.

Under Mr. Swinton's direction, the Art Centre became a veritable hive of activity. He extended visiting hours, introduced record-listening sessions during the noon hours, arranged regular Friday-evening programs with panel discussions, demonstrations, and visiting lecturers, organized dozens of exciting exhibitions and wrote and talked about them. He relied on his wife, Alice, for secretarial assistance.

Mr. Swinton had an impact on the members of the art community, too, for he recognized the need to establish professional standards. The artists, with a few exceptions, had been content to function without a society of their own to watch over standards. One of the stated functions of the Saskatchewan Arts Board, which was planned as a servicing body, had been to help with the creation of a Saskatchewan Arts Council, which would act in the interests of the artists, but the board had taken no action in that direction. The university had been given the green light to develop its art department so that students could be taught methods of teaching art, and Dr. Snelgrove had appointed Nikola Bjelajac, a Wisconsin-trained artist, to give practical instruction.

With an art school in the making and a professional artist at the head of the Art Centre, the time seemed right to form a group which could sit in judgment on its membership and could act, as the Ontario Society of Artists had acted for years, as an arbiter of quality. A few Saskatoon artists, therefore, joined together as The Prospectors. The group was short-lived, but it helped to underline the recognition that local artists were gaining, and their awareness of their responsibility to the community to produce art of a high quality.

Robert Hurley, whose work at the laboratory left him little enough time for sketching and painting, remained aloof from all the discussions and activities, except for attendance at the centre for events which particularly attracted him. Yet he benefited from the public's aroused interest in art, for the demand for his water colors grew month by month and year by year. His art work consumed more and more of his free time, and his family was to learn what a jealous mistress painting, like the other arts, could be.

The sketching expeditions, which he had always enjoyed, became more important to him when he was confined indoors a great deal of the time. Not only were they necessary to replenish his stock of shorthand nature notes but they also refreshed him physically and spiritually. Most of the trips were to familiar spots around Saskatoon—Sutherland Beach, Yorath Island, Beaver Creek, Cranberry Flats, Clark's Crossing, Pike Lake, all within an hour's drive from Sutherland. One day, when he and Mr. Wickenden and Mashel were on their way to Yorath Island, a thunderstorm developed, and Wickenden, knowing that the lower river road would become impassable, stopped near the Quaker Oats plant and the three artists took out their sketching materials and worked in the car. Each of them chose a different approach for their paintings, with Hurley opting for the realistic (Plate XIII).

When Hurley and Wickenden could manage to match a few days away from work, they would take off for more distant fields, Hurley with his harmonica in his pocket and Wickenden with a song on his lips and his fishing tackle in the trunk.

On one such trip they went as far as Battleford where they stayed in a tourist camp and sketched in the wild Eagle Hills country. They returned by way of Radisson to Langham where; at Bill's invitation, they stayed for a few days at the Perehudoff farm not far from the Borden Bridge over the North Saskatchewan River. In earlier days the area had been a favored picnic grounds for Saskatonians. It boasts a marvelous view from the river heights, and great stretches of sandy banks which, when the river is low, extend as sandbars practically across the river bed in intriguing patterns. Each spring driftwood, carried downstream by the ice, is piled up on the banks, providing inviting patterns for artists and aromatic fuel for city fireplaces.

While Hurley was busy at the lab and off on his sketching trips, things weren't going well at the Art Centre. Memberships had increased but so had expenses, and the directors were finding it difficult to pay Mr. Swinton's salary. The artists came to the rescue, as they had once before when the centre was short of funds, and donated hundreds of pictures and pieces of sculpture for a public auction. A. J. Trotter looked after the arrangements and had to write to Mr. Hurley a second time requesting pictures, for the collection of paintings for sale, Mr. Trotter said, wouldn't seem complete without some Hurleys in it.

It wasn't that Hurley objected to donating paintings. He simply had none to donate. As was to happen several times during the following decade, he had scraped the bottom of the Hurley water-color box. However, he dashed off some "quickies" for the purpose of the sale.

Mr. Swinton, who had been anxious to continue his studies, resigned as curator and departed for New York. The first centre closed in April of 1949, unable to pay its way when the rent was raised. So much of an impression had it made, however, that another location was found—in the arcade of the King George Hotel—and the centre was reopened on October the fourteenth, 1949.

The centre had to operate on a shoestring, and the shoestring was critically frayed at the end of the first three months. Some public-spirited citizens guaranteed operating expenses until a new city grant would be available, and a group of young women came to its financial aid by promoting the first Beaux Arts Ball. It was the first time that the community had come to the aid of art, and the artists certainly went to the aid of the ball by turning the ballroom of the Bessborough Hotel into a fanciful world. From 1949 until the opening of the Mendel Gallery, the Saskatoon Art Centre, under the direction of Mrs. Lea Collins, continued to serve the community and the artists in it.

The Mendels had come to Saskatoon at the beginning of the 1940 decade.

The Siftons came towards its end. Clifford M. Sifton, as editor of the *Star-Phoenix,* gave unstinted support to all the arts in the city. Geraldine Sifton was the prime moving force behind the three Beaux Arts Balls that were held. Together, they were patrons of art, encouraging the local artists, buying their pictures, and stirring up interest in their work. There were Bill Perehudoff murals above their mantel and on the staircase wall; and there was a Hurley water color in their den.

The forties were lively years in the city's art world, and rewarding years for Robert Hurley, whose reputation was growing by bounds. But, for Hurley, they were nothing compared to the following decade.

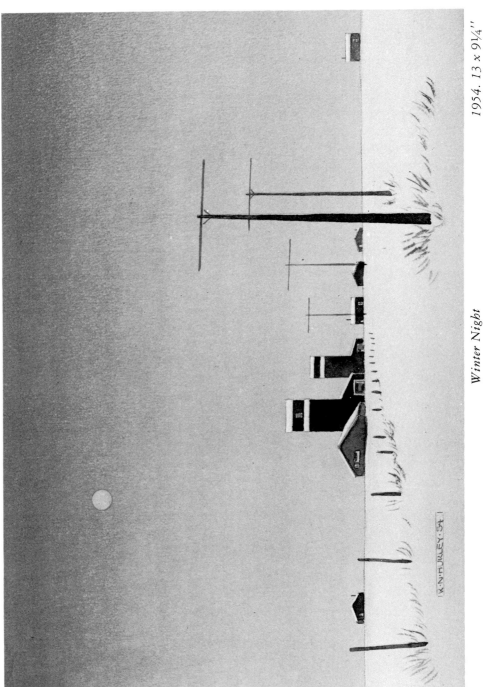

Winter Night

1954. 13 x 9¼"

10

The Illustrious Decade

THE PERMANENT DISPLAY in the University of Saskatchewan bookstore, the two-man show with Hilda Stewart in the Saskatoon Art Centre, the activities at the centre, the stream of visitors through the plant pathology laboratory, the patronage of the arts by prominent Saskatoon families, all these factors contributed to publicizing the work of Robert Hurley. The reverse side of the coin, however, was by no means blank. Hurley's paintings of the Saskatchewan landscape contributed more than can be measured to stirring up public interest in the work of local artists, and to opening the eyes of the public to the beauties around them, from the obvious splendor of a flaming sunset to the still magic of snow-blanketed fields in the moonlight. The public wanted more and more and more Hurley water colors of familiar prairie sights, until the demand almost overwhelmed the artist. Perhaps even more than any publicity he ever received, even to the sum total of it all, Hurley's paintings were their own best advertisement.

Hurley was certainly never neglected as far as publicity was concerned, for the story of his life—from slums to success—had a wide romantic appeal, and the unique prairie quality of his landscapes had an equally wide pictorial appeal, both of which made good copy for writers and commentators.

In the May, 1950, issue of *The Union Farmer,* the house organ of the Saskatchewan Farmers' Union, Dr. Charles Lightbody, of the university's history department, contributed an article, "Robert Newton Hurley, Painter of the Prairies." Hurley considered it "by far the most complimentary article ever done about my paintings." He had done a painting for the journal's cover, and the editor, Diana Wright, had borrowed two cuts from the *Star-Phoenix* to illustrate the article.

"It is not for drawing or composition," Dr. Lightbody wrote, "but for his great control of color that he is remarkable and especially for his mastery of washes, in which colors blend to create new colors."

Dr. Lightbody was the first writer to compare Hurley's use of the grain elevator as a prairie symbol to the use of the windmill by Dutch painters. Many writers have followed suit. Dr. Lightbody was also the first writer to label Hurley as the "painter of the Prairies." And many since have used the expression.

Dr. Lightbody, one of Yorkton's distinguished sons, arranged an exhibit of Hurley's paintings in that Saskatchewan center, and wrote to Hurley in July that the show was handsomely mounted in the Royal Bank. Many of the paintings in the display were purchased by the bank and by citizens of Yorkton. For this, and for later shows, Mr. Hurley's problem wasn't the finding of a gallery or a sponsor for an exhibition but the keeping on hand of enough work to send to groups and galleries that requested exhibits.

Requests for paintings to put on display came from many sources. Rural groups, such as the Landis Homemakers' Club, and agricultural organizations, such as the Saskatchewan Farmers' Union and the Saskatchewan Wheat Pool, asked for his prairie scenes to mount displays at their annual meetings. When national societies held their conventions in Saskatoon, organizers sought Hurley paintings to hang in order to show visitors from other parts of the country how Saskatchewan looked through the eyes of one of its most successful interpreters. In 1955, for instance, Mrs. A. L. Caldwell arranged an exhibit of Hurley paintings for the convention of the National Council of Women, held at the university, and sold five of his water colors on the spot.

Public institutions, such as the Winnipeg Art Gallery, Regina College, and the Glenbow Foundation in Calgary, and privately owned galleries, such as the Dominion Gallery in Montreal, James Art Studio in Saskatoon, and the Burlington Art Shop in Edmonton, arranged displays of Hurley's water colors. And exhibitions were planned by individuals who felt that persons in other centers would be interested in seeing the work of the very original and regional artist, Robert Hurley. One such individual was Count Serge de Fleury, French consul at Winnipeg, who was so attracted by Hurley's pictures when he visited the artist at the laboratory in November, 1951, that he asked permission to arrange for a display in Winnipeg; another was Mr. Furniss of Port Alberni, British Columbia, who asked for some prairie landscapes to show in that city.

And there was always Mr. Hurley's own stamping ground, the University of Saskatchewan. The university's rapid expansion in postwar years, which accelerated during the 1950's, changed the face of the campus radically. The University Hospital, a massive, stone-walled complex which blocked off the western horizon, was opened in 1955 and was associated with the College of Medicine which had been established in 1952. In 1952, at the request of the Medical College, Hurley loaned twenty painings for an exhibition in its library. In 1951, the university librarian had selected five Hurley paintings to pin up in the library. When the library was moved from College Building to the Murray Memorial Library in 1956, space in attractive surroundings made the displays of Hurley water colors more effective. Much to Mr. Hurley's delight, he was given permission to take whatever magazines and books he wanted from the library discards at the time of the move, and he added several travel books to his collection and stocked up on color reproductions for his scrapbooks.

Hurley paintings were also included in displays without the knowledge of the artist. In February of 1955 he received a catalogue of an exhibition of Canadian art held at Fortnum and Mason's in London, sponsored by the Ontario Government. Four Hurleys, the property of Graham Spry, the agent general for Saskatchewan, were included in the display and, much to Mr. Hurley's amusement, were described in an English newspaper as "desert scenes from Saskatchewan."

Diana and Jim Wright had taken Mr. Spry to look at Hurley's paintings in the late 1940's when the agent general was visiting Saskatoon, and he had bought seven. Back in Saskatchewan House in London, England, he had them hung along the stairwell, calling the display Dawn to Dusk on the Prairies. Mrs. Wright, who saw them in their London setting, reports that they were greatly admired by visitors to Saskatchewan House, many of whom wanted to know where they could obtain paintings by Hurley.

Each year, the Saskatchewan Arts Board purchased several paintings from the provincial exhibitions in order to build up a permanent collection which could be circulated around the smaller Saskatchewan centers. In 1952, Hurley's "Winter" was one of the paintings purchased, and the number of times it was on display, along with later purchases, is a matter of conjecture.

Imperial Oil officials visited the lab and bought three to add to that company's collection of art. A representative of the Ford Foundation bought two to send to India. Mr. and Mrs. F. F. MacDermid selected a water color to send to the Honorable T. C. "Tommy" Davis, the Canadian Ambassador at Bonn, West Germany, a transaction which particularly appealed to the artist because he had worked for the MacDermids during his Idylwyld gardening days; and the painting probably appealed to Mr. Davis, for he had been raised in Prince Albert and had served as attorney general of Saskatchewan for some years under a Liberal government. In 1951, Mr. Hurley received a commission to paint a Saskatchewan landscape for the Canadian Club in New York City.

Hurley paintings were getting around the world. How far the list could be extended, no one knows, least of all Mr. Hurley who has been constantly surprised by news of where his water colors have ended up. As a great many were bought as presentation gifts for persons leaving for destinations unknown, the pictures are as widely scattered as if they had been blown away by Saskatchewan winds.

One fact is certain: Except for the two years that Hurley submitted paintings to the Ontario Society of Artists, in 1938 and 1939, and for the few years that he sent pictures to the Manitoba Art Association, he has made no effort to have his paintings accepted by any association or displayed in any gallery. He has simply filled requests for pictures to be displayed, whenever it was possible for him to do so. As late as March, 1972, he had to turn down a request from the picture loan department of the Art Gallery of Greater Victoria. He would have liked to have had some pictures included in the loan collection in Victoria, a city where prairie residents like to retire, but he had only four or five available and of those, two had been promised to a Calgary lawyer.

Mr. Hurley has completely lost track of the number of paintings he has sold or given away. At an average of five a week for thirty years—a conservative estimate—the number comes to 7,800! In addition he has done hundreds of small landscapes, flower studies, and abstracts. If he had started painting before he was twenty, as his boyhood hero Turner had, he might have rivaled the figure of 19,000 paintings and drawings left by Turner to the English nation.

It wasn't until about 1970 that Mrs. Hurley realized that she owned TWO finished Hurleys, not even as many as the Queen of England, who has five. Since then she has made off with a few sketches and smaller paintings, but she hasn't managed to add to her collection of landscapes, for Bob doesn't create as many paintings as he once did—only about two a week now and they are usually in response to a specific demand. In a letter dated March the twenty-sixth, 1972, his seventy-eighth birthday, he said: "I am still reviving many of those pencil sketches done between 1933 to 1943. I have about 60 now in album. Isabella 'swipes' a few, to store upstairs in the metal trunk."

The Queen of England is partly to blame for Isabella turning into a "thief."

On Sunday, October the fourteenth, 1951, Dr. Snelgrove arrived at the Hurley home on Railway Avenue in a state of great excitement. He had been commissioned by Premier T. C. Douglas to select paintings to be presented to Princess Elizabeth and Prince Philip when they visited Regina—and they were on their way! Dr. Snelgrove selected fifteen, and rushed them to the C.N. station to be shipped on the midnight train.

It was sheer luck—Mr. Hurley would call it a miracle—that he had enough paintings to enable Dr. Snelgrove to make a good selection, for he had painted only six during the first two weeks of October. He had found the work at the lab more strenuous than usual as it involved filling the soil bin in readiness for winter, and cutting and bagging the green clover on the plots, and he had used up most of his spare energy getting his own garden cleaned up before the first snow. Also, he had gone out more than was his custom, attending sessions of an Apostolic Pentecostal Mission over the Thanksgiving weekend, going to the Art Centre to hear a lecture on Western artists on the twelfth, and watching a religious color film on the Saturday before the selection. He reported in his diary on two occasions that he was "tired and cranky."

On Wednesday, October the seventeenth, he had this to report in his diary:

"This has been the GREAT day for me. The ex-hobo, ex-lumberjack, one-time camp cookee, relief recipient, good for nothing, rolling stone, farm hand, and present lackey to a science laboratory, now painter to H. R. H. Princess Elizabeth and Philip, Duke of Edinboro (sic). Dr. Snelgrove snatched me from my errand to the physics lab to hear the broadcast from our capital city, Regina. The premier gave a fine clear to-the-point address of welcome which the Princess responded to in a sweet vibrant voice. It was all so lovely. My, what a thrill when I heard my paintings were presented to their royal highnesses." (Hon. J. H. Brocklebank, Minister of Natural Resources, had made the presentation.)

Everywhere Mr. Hurley went for the next couple of weeks he was swamped with congratulations and with requests for paintings. Four paintings, representing each of the seasons, had been presented to the royal couple, and it became the vogue for patrons to ask for four paintings. He was short of winter scenes, but fortunately, on the twenty-fifth, there was a heavy downfall of snow. Hurley made a memory sketch of the snow at dawn before he started off to work, and later in the week painted three scenes from the one sketch, all of which he liked for their "simplicity and clean color."

His sales for the first week in November totaled $217, "not bad," he wrote in his diary, "for a few potboilers."

On November the fifteenth, he received a check for $200 for the royal paintings, and he proudly went off to the bank to deposit it. Fifty dollars a painting was the most he had received up to that time, and more than he ever brought himself to ask.

By the end of the month he was scraping the bottom of the box again. He considered applying for a week's leave of absence to paint, but somehow he managed to paint enough during the evenings to keep pace with the demand and was at the lab during the daytime to receive the visitors who came in increasing numbers. One evening he painted two "quickies" between eight and ten, and a few evenings later he painted three water colors in an hour and a half. His sales for the first week of December totaled $225.

Mr. Hurley had, and still has, a lovely way of saying "thank you." On the first Sunday in December he missed his bus for church, and after watching the goldfish, listening to the canary, and playing with their dog, Paddy, for a time, he decided to transgress from his custom of not painting on

Sunday. He worked out a "marvelously delicate sunset color-scheme in rose, green, gray, purple"—his Christmas gift for Premier Douglas.

The presentation of his paintings to the Princess and the resulting mad rush for his water colors gave Hurley's spirits a tremendous boost. He was still tired, mostly because he had to work too hard under the pressure of the demand, but he was not "cranky." Instead, a feeling of joyful excitement emanates from his diary, as in the following entry written on December the eleventh after he had attended the annual carol festival in which their daughter Alice had participated: "Ideas for painting flow in with a floodlike surge. Last night a full moon peek-a-booing through gray clouds with indigo sky way behind in the mysterious abyss of space. A bright gem of a distant star flashing through the holes in the gray ghostly clouds. Did quickie." Since he was busy painting pictures of the seasons, he was happy when he happened to tune in to Vivaldi's "Four Seasons"—"to me about the loveliest music possible."

Mr. Hurley often referred to his paintings as "quickies." By "quickie" he meant a scene painted in a hurry in an effort to capture his impression of a moment. His "quickies" were on-the-spot recordings of his responses. He always enjoyed painting "quickies" and often he himself would be surprised by some quality of beauty he had been able to express.

He also often referred to his paintings as "potboilers." By "potboiler" he meant a painting worked up from a memory sketch or pencil sketch. For instance, on December the nineteenth he noted that at ten thirty in the morning the wife of a local judge had visited the lab and bought a "potboiler." "This," he wrote, "is the fourth painting done from the same source material, by changing perspective, composition and minor details. I turn the trick each time into a fairly satisfying Saskatchewan landscape." He noted that Dr. Carlyle King, then of the English department and later a vice-principal of the university, had bought the first painting from the sketch.

Sometimes, when the weather prevented sketching trips or when he was simply too tired to make the effort, he would stay at home and work from his pile of pencil and crayon notes. "I seem to have the happy faculty of re-creating from the slightest thumbnail sketch," he wrote on one occasion when he felt too weak to work outdoors.

However, he could also grow impatient when he was forced by the demand for his landscapes to paint too many "potboilers." "I am getting weary working from stale pencil sketches," he wrote at the end of one long winter when the reflections of the Sutherland elevators in the snow water lured him out of the house.

"Potboilers," he complained to himself, "are the kind that sell." He wasn't always satisfied with his "potboilers." On completing eight water colors when he was confined to the house for a couple of days in early 1955, he noted that "four are of a good quality." Usually he was as good a judge as anyone of his paintings, and very often when he felt that they were poor or mediocre, he had painted them when he was feeling rotten.

He thought of his water colors that sold as the "usual stuff." "Usual stuff" meant "elevators, sunset sky, telephone poles." To the criticism that his paintings were only repetitions of each other, his answer was that that well-known theme "allows infinity of variations, both in color and composition. Degas painted ballet dancers with feverish ferocity. Picasso has juggled incessantly with cubes and paint, and I read of an Italian artist who twenty years ago threw a party and has been painting the empty wine bottles for inspiration since."

He was sincere in his defense of his "potboilers" against the charge of repetitiousness, but he sometimes expressed disappointment that the public preferred them to his other paintings. "Funny," he wrote, March the first, 1957, "how the public go for these telephone pole studies, plus a grain elevator or two, plus a vast sky with clouds, all within a 10 by 14 sheet. So much contained in So little."

He could point the finger of blame, of course, only at himself. Of all artists, he had captured the quality of the Prairies that had the most universal appeal. He had created the demand through his talent as a painter of the sky.

To the phrase "So much contained in So little," he might well have added "for So little." Hurley paintings were also popular with the public because of prices. The prices were fantastically, almost ridiculously, low!

What could be called the "depression complex" took a long time to disappear in the Canadian West, a region which had been more severely hit for a longer time than most other parts of the country. Most salaries were frozen during the 1930's, and World War II was well advanced before any increases were granted. Individuals who had been badly victimized by the hard times, like Hurley, took many years to get into step with the affluent society that developed after the war. Some never did.

Hurley had been familiar with poverty since his childhood, and the way of life he had been forced to follow had not helped him to develop any business sense. When he sold his first pictures for a few dollars each, he marveled that he had a little cash to buy some materials to paint more pictures. At that, he had to conceal most of his sales or the relief office would have cut off his family's monthly cash allowance of five dollars. When his paintings began to sell in quantity after he started work at the laboratory, he was content to accept anywhere from five dollars to twenty-five dollars for a water color. A person who had fifteen dollars to buy a painting would likely leave the lab with the painting of his choice, even though Hurley had put a twenty- or twenty-five-dollar price tag on it. He simply wasn't a salesman.

Mr. Hurley's poverty-born concept of the value of money only partly explained his attitude about the value of his paintings, however, for he was motivated, when setting a price on them, by his belief that his talent for water-color painting was God-given. He believed that he had no right to charge prices which were beyond the reach of the most humble. He could have made a distinction, perhaps, between the rich and the poor and adjusted his prices accordingly, for there were many who would have willingly paid more than he asked; but to do so, for him, would have been a distasteful form of discrimination.

Just as his admirers' preference for his "potboilers" puzzled him at times, so at other times he was frustrated by his admirers' encroachment on his scarce and precious painting time.

"I should have an agent," he wrote one Saturday night, weary after a day of showing his paintings to visitors when he would rather have been painting.

An agent could have manipulated prices for him to bring him a higher return; and an agent could have protected him from visitors who took too long to make their decisions. But an agent would also have robbed him of what was really one of his chief delights—meeting the persons who wanted to buy his paintings; and an agent would have deprived his public of one of their pleasures—meeting and talking with the artist. He loved showing his work, most of the time, and he loved being able to send people away happy with their water colors. The experience of the men in the laboratory came nearer to revealing Hurley's attitude to people who admired his paintings than his occasional bursts of impatience. They had to be careful to restrain their praise or they would find themselves the owners of another Hurley, for it delighted him to give his paintings away.

He had agents, of a kind. Friends like Gladys Ellard, the stenographer in the laboratory, and Eileen Child, who worked in the lab during the summer months, often showed his paintings to callers when he was away or busy. Miss Child, who worked during the winter as a seed analyst in the Federal Building downtown, often took a dozen or fifteen Hurleys to the downtown office where they went "like hotcakes."

There were many persons who believed that Hurley didn't price his paintings according to their value and who chided him for being too easy. Not only did he practically give his work away, even at the highest price of about twenty-five dollars, but he would go to endless trouble packaging and mailing the pictures for out-of-town patrons without any extra charge. People offered him advice about how to make more money from his work. R. H. Macdonald, of *The Western Producer,* for one, suggested that he send some color slides to a calendar business in Toronto which paid from fifty to two hundred dollars for suitable kodachromes, but Hurley wasn't any more interested in seeking lucrative returns than he was in arranging exhibits. In a nutshell, he was too busy painting to become a businessman.

When asked, in 1972, if he had kept on producing "potboilers" for the money they brought in, his answer was that it was the demand for them, not the money he received, that had moved him to paint typical prairie scenes when he would have liked more time for other types of painting. He admitted, quite candidly, that the demand flattered his ego, particularly when it came from highly educated, distinguished members of the community. By the mid-1950's, Hurley was a great success as a painter, but even his success couldn't rid him of the deep feeling of insecurity bred in him by an unhappy childhood home and a poor education.

Hurley's prairie landscapes were no more repetitious than the country he depicted. Thousands of travelers across the plains have considered themselves to be in the midst of a monotomous wasteland. Hurley's own reaction to the Prairies when he reached Milden in 1923 was a sense of the utter desolation of the scene. But for those who have eyes to see, the Prairies offer an infinite variety of patterns and rhythms and colors, subtly different from minute to minute as the winds change the cloud face of the sky and dramatically different from dawn to sunset and from the gold of summer to the winter snows. Hurley, an original and sensitive regional painter, opened the eyes of prairie dwellers. For many, the Prairies began to look like a Hurley landscape!

To own a Hurley landscape was to own a part of the Prairies, and the relatively small size made it possible to take or send a part of the Prairies anywhere in the world.

As the university and city expanded during the 1950's, the demand for Hurley paintings kept pace. Buyers, almost literally, flocked to the lab and to his home. They came singly and often bought several, and they came in groups to select one as a presentation gift for a dozen and one reasons—promotion, retirement, wedding, Christmas, birthday, anniversary, and suchlike.

A group of Girl Guides, with a carefully hoarded five dollars, came for a Hurley to present to their teacher, and he helped them with their selection. A member of the soils department called to select a painting for a departing stenographer, with ten dollars collected by passing around the hat. The Technical Collegiate teachers presented one of his paintings to the retiring head of the night school program; the Separate School Board presented two to a retiring member in recognition of her long service; the law society gave a Hurley to an old lawyer when he decided to stop practicing. Some of the presentations made items in the local newspaper; others were quietly noted by Hurley in his diary. Teachers, lawyers, doctors, bankers, journalists, politicians, ministers, musicians, scientists, farmers, nurses, technicians, librarians, students, stenographers, housewives, merchants—all are mentioned as receiving and most of them as giving Hurleys as gifts; and no doubt the list could be lengthened to include practically every occupation under the sun if it were possible to track down all the Hurleys that were presented.

Many individuals collected Hurley paintings until their homes or offices took on the appearance of Hurley displays. His diary entry for Monday, May the second, 1955, reads: "Request from Mrs. E. W. Barootes of Regina—this started a continuing patronage, resulting in the doctor's home and offices becoming almost a one-man museum of Hurley prairie interpretations."

Over the years, Dr. and Mrs. Barootes have bought more than one hundred Hurleys. They have kept a score or so for themselves and have presented the others to friends and relations when occasions called for gifts. Like so many Hurley patrons, Doctor Barootes found it hard to persuade Mr. Hurley to take enough money for the paintings, so the doctor left the business arrangements to his wife, for Hurley would hesitate before arguing with the fairer sex.

In Saskatoon, the office of Dr. A. L. Caldwell was similarly decorated. The men at the laboratory, who had the good fortune to be the first to see most of the new Hurleys, built up sizable collections, the Russells, for instance, owning fourteen.

The exceptional fact is that the private collections which boast more than a half dozen Hurley paintings are not exceptional.

Not all the persons who collected Hurley paintings purchased them from the artist. Such a one is A. J. E. Child, president and chief executive officer of Burns Foods Limited, Calgary. Mr. Child, who lived in Saskatoon for a few years in the early 1960's, has never met Hurley but owns over thirty of his paintings. When *The Western Producer's* Mr. Macdonald learned of Mr. Child's collection, he wrote and asked how his interest had been aroused. Mr. Child replied:

"I first saw one of his paintings on a calendar in Saskatoon, about 1961. The stylistic treatment of prairie scenes appealed to me very much and I began to buy his paintings, especially when I could find some of the older ones. Now I have over 30.

"It is only about a year that I have been in touch with him by correspondence, after I found out about his situation. It is simply a case that I think he is a very fine artist and I would like to help him. There is possibly a strong personal appeal in his paintings for me because I am very fond of Saskatchewan. I like the wide and bleak spaces of the prairies. The land is a challenge that brings out the strengths and weaknesses of people. The emptiness is a relief from crowded cities and complex business problems."

Perhaps the most unusual display of Hurley paintings was staged by Mr. Hurley himself in his hospital sick room in 1955. He was so restless and uncomfortable after surgery that in an effort to cheer him up his family decorated his room with his paintings. His stock was at a low ebb and there were only a dozen or so small ones left. Within a few days he was ready to be discharged, by which time many of the paintings had been bought by hospital personnel.

On September the twenty-fifth, the day after his discharge, he painted his first scene since becoming sick—a nocturne, which was bought the following day by the Quota Club. By the end of the month he had painted twelve water colors, and he recorded that he seemed to be painting more meticulously than before his operation and with cleaner tints. The enforced rest had obviously provided him with new enthusiasm.

The procession of visitors to the laboratory and to the Hurley home took on the nature of a pilgrimage as all those with an interest in art and those who pretended to an interest in art felt drawn to call on the water-colorist whose paintings spelled the Prairies. It was fitting, therefore, that one of Hurley's paintings should be chosen to be presented to the Rev. Geoffrey F. Fisher, whose title, Archbishop of Canterbury, was associated with the oldest of English pilgrimages. Hurley's diary is a blank for he month of October, 1954, when the Archbishop of Canterbury visited Saskatoon, but it is not difficult to imagine the "thrill" of the artist at the thought of one of his water colors hanging in Lambeth Palace.

He was always pleased when he learned that his pictures were being taken or sent to England. Dr. Chinn's lab at the greenhouse was fixed up as a display room for Hurley paintings on a Sunday in early May, 1956, when Magistrate B. M. Wakeling had made an appointment to bring his cousin, Air Chief Marshall Sir John Baker, to meet Mr. Hurley and to see his work. Mrs. Wakeling had bought the occasional Hurley water color before that time, and Sir John, attracted by the artist's interpretation of the landscape, had expressed a desire to get a couple for his own collection.

The meeting with Sir John Baker was an exciting one for Mr. Hurley, for one of his favorite hymns in the Anglican hymn book, "The King of Love My Shepherd Is" (539), was written by Sir John's father, Rev. Sir

H. W. Baker, in 1868. Mr Hurley sings this hymn to many tunes, but favors an air from Mozart's "Don Giovanni."

Stories about Mr. Hurley's painting career reflected and promoted his increasing recognition. In an article in *Canadian Art* in 1944, he was named as one of the outstanding landscape painters of Saskatchewan, and the same magazine carried a story on him by Dr. Lightbody in the Christmas-New Year's issue of 1950-51, a reiteration of the article printed in *The Union Farmer* earlier. Mention of his work appeared with regularity in the *Saskatoon Star-Phoenix* as reports on the annual fall shows at the Art Centre and the annual provincial exhibitions were printed. His picture appeared on the front page of the *Star-Phoenix*—a page usually reserved at that time for news of world-shaking importance—in the account of the presentation of his paintings to the Princess in 1951; and he noted with regret that the cut used was fifteen years old.

In January, 1952, Idabelle Melville, a CBC broadcaster, gave a six-minute talk on Hurley and his work on the "Voice of Canada" program, reviewing the drama of his rise from poverty to success and highlighting the royal presentation. A few weeks after the presentation to the Archbishop of Canterbury, Dan Worden, of radio station CKOM in Saskatoon, taped an interview with the artist which was broadcast on March the twenty-eighth, 1955, on his daily "People You Meet" program. "I got a big thrill tonight, hearing my own voice," Hurley told his diary, noting down the details of his life which had been included in the interview.

Even when Hurley or art wasn't the main topic for a story, his name often crept into print. A year or so before the town of Sutherland was amalgamated with the city of Saskatoon in late 1955, an article appeared in the local press about the character of the town from the time it had been incorporated in 1912. It was reported that the town's population was about 1,000, living within an area of 3,500 acres, and that 95 per cent of the population depended on the rail industry. The final paragraph announced: "One of Sutherland's most famous residents is Robert Hurley, an artist who is well known for his water colors of the Prairie scene."

Articles, spaced a year or so apart, appeared in the *Winnipeg Free Press Weekly,* the *Calgary Farm and Ranch Review,* and in the magazine section of the *Toronto Globe and Mail,* all written by Stanley Obodiac, who had become interested in Hurley's work as early as 1950 when it was shown in the Royal Bank at Yorkton. All the articles were based on information about Hurley which Mr. Obodiac had gathered while working on a book about the artist, which was to be entitled "Robert Hurley, The Prairie Painter." The book was not published, but Mr. Obodiac's journalistic work helped to broaden the interest in Hurley's paintings.

Hurley not only sketched railway tracks, he sketched on them, finding they provided a good back rest.

In 1957 a team from the Canadian Broadcasting Corporation invaded Sutherland and took sequences of Isabella in the rhubarb patch and Hurley at the lab and sketching by the railroad tracks, which were edited for a fifteen-minute show on "Country Calendar."

In addition to the articles and programs, reproductions of Hurley paintings used by publishers and printers and business firms brought publicity for his work.

The first time a Hurley painting was used as an illustration for a book jacket was in 1947 for Mr. McCourt's *Music at the Close,* which shared the Ryerson Fiction Award that year with Will Bird's *Judgment Glen.* It was a snow scene, with two rows of telephone poles lining the road leading to a small prairie town and its lone elevator, under a bright yellow sky fading into pale lemon and shading off into warm gray. Riverview, the typical little prairie town in the novel, could well have been modeled on the town in the distance of the Hurley scene.

The latest dust jacket to carry a reproduction of a Hurley is the one for the new edition of *The Carlton Trail* by Dr. Russell, first printed in

1955 by the Prairie Book Division of *The Western Producer.* It presents a panoramic view of the Prairies, with a little slough in the distance and a Red River cart in the foreground. When Dr. Russell was gathering the material for his book, he often drove Mr. Hurley some miles east of Sutherland to the vicinity of Patience Lake—now the site of a potash mine—and Hurley would sketch the countryside with a view to adding Indian encampments, carts, and travelers along the historic trail.

In 1967, a reproduction of a Hurley painting, "Prairie Dawn," was used as a frontispiece for *Proud Heritage,* a history of the Conquest, Saskatchewan, region compiled by the Centennial Committee. The picture was painted expressly for the book at the request of Lenore Sills, and donated by the artist.

Requests for paintings for reproduction purposes came in steadily during the crowded years after 1951. In 1952, Frank Lovell and Doug Cherry, officials of the Saskatchewan Alumni Association, visited the lab to select a painting for the cover of "The Green and White," the alumni news magazine. All graduates who were on the mailing list of the association received regular copies of the magazine, which meant that the featured painting by Hurley traveled vast distances, for Saskatchewan graduates are notorious for their tendency to scatter around the world.

In 1953, a Saskatoon automotive firm, Bowman Brothers, used a Hurley landscape on its Christmas card; in 1954, it was the Stovel-Advocate Press that wanted paintings to use on calendars and cards; in 1955, Dr. Snelgrove selected a water color for the Saskatchewan Government's calendar. The Saskatoon Art Centre kept on hand a supply of hasti-notes and Christmas cards with designs or paintings by several local artists, including Hurley. The Royal Trust Company reproduced a landscape on its 1962 calendar, and the cover for the *Sun Life Review* for July, 1966, sported a Hurley.

Radio station CHAB in Moose Jaw, in 1955, used part of a Hurley painting as a decorative letterhead on its business stationery.

If Mr. Hurley had had a business manager, he would probably have become a wealthy man.

On March the twenty-sixth, 1956, his sixty-second birthday, he commented on what a lot of history he had accumulated, and added up his blessings, starting with his family and continuing ". . . about $1,500 in savings, nice home paid for—lovely quiet home location. Huge and prolific garden—100 yards square surrounded by kind, quiet neighbors and within one-half mile of the open prairie. Record library, canary, goldfish, house plants. My art, stamp collection, good books and many friends."

Mr. Hurley considered himself to be a wealthy man!

The faculty of the University of Saskatchewan made up the main bulk of Hurley patrons with hardly any department of any college not represented in the names that dot the Hurley diary. Some names appear more frequently than others, but to single out any from the general list would distort their significance. Mr. Hurley was always as delighted by the interest shown by young graduates as he was impressed by the importance of distinguished callers. As the fifties advanced there was no letup in the demand, for the university faculty grew in proportion to the university's physical expansion. And if the demand had wavered, it would have received a boost from another presentation to Royalty, in July, 1958.

In April of that year the Saskatchewan Power Corporation commissioned Mr. Hurley to paint its new power plant, which was to be called the Queen Elizabeth Power Plant and was to be activated by a remote-control switch by the Queen when she visited Saskatoon in July. There were those who expressed the opinion that a painting of a power plant was hardly an appropriate gift for a queen, but they were persons who had forgotten or hadn't known—such as one English newspaper—that Saskatoon's power plant had long been an outdoor model for a number of local artists. In 1934, Mr. Hurley, applying the water-color technique he had learned from the Richmond-Littlejohns book, had used the power house for his first landscape painting in Saskatoon, had submitted it to the local fair, and had won third prize in the landscape section.

The new power plant was not only a more attractive pictorial challenge than the local plant, but it was also situated on a stretch of the river bank which had long been one of Hurley's favorite sketching localities (Plate XV). It was on the west bank of the river, south of the Grand Trunk Pacific bridge (now the C.N.R.)—the Yorath Island region. There were sandbars and rocks, water and sky to be used for the setting. The commissioned painting was to be fairly realistic, but Mr. Hurley knew how to indicate bricks without counting them.

He painted a number of versions of the plant. The SPC bought four and chose one of the four for the presentation which was made on July the twenty-second by the Honorable Russ Brown, Minister of Travel and Information, and David Cass-Beggs, head of the Power Corporation.

A few days later Hurley received a telephone call from Esmond Butler, who was press secretary for the Royal tour. He was phoning from the Royal coach, which had been pulled off on a siding several miles from Regina while the Queen took tea with a "model" farmer, and he requested Mr. Hurley to send some paintings to him at Buckingham Palace. Cecil James, of James Art Studio, packaged half a dozen landscapes for Mr. Hurley and sent them on their way. Mr. Butler sold a couple to the staff at Buckingham Palace and kept the rest for himself.

The decade which began with the fanfare of the presentation of four paintings to Royalty ended with a bang during the official visit of Governor General Georges Vanier and Mrs. Vanier to Saskatoon in 1960. There was much excitement in the Hurley home when the viceregal limousine delivered visitors to look at the paintings. The same Mr. Butler who had been with the Queen's 1958 tour, and his bride, bought two prairie landscapes and an abstract of sandpipers in the grass, and J. A. J. Lajeunesse, military aide to the Governor General and one-time teacher of French to Prince Charles, bought two landscapes and two abstracts of fish.

There was nothing abstract about Mr. Hurley's joy, and he was particularly delighted that his abstracts had shared some honors with his landscapes.

11

The Fun of Painting

THE FOURTEEN-YEAR-OLD BOY who had hopefully submitted an advertising design to a tea company in London was not lost in the forty-year-old man who won first prize for the flower study he entered in the Saskatoon Exhibition in 1934. His interest in the grain of a piece of wood, the shape of a seed under a microscope, the outline of a snowflake, which he registered in the first diary he kept, accelerated as his powers of observation sharpened through use and as his reading introduced him to more of the wonders of nature.

The necessity to experiment with homemade colors on any available type of paper, during the 1930's, led to a continuing interest in experimentation with different methods of applying paint and in using a wide variety of subject matter for purposes of design. This interest in experimentation combined with his fascination with design are behind all the paintings which he refers to as abstracts. The designs for his prairie landscapes were handed to him on the platter of the sky; the designs for his abstracts were of his own choosing and creating. His landscapes, even those which were close to abstracts, called on his talent as a water-colorist and on his power of observation; his abstracts, even those which were close to being representational, called on his inventive and creative abilities.

As early as 1938 it was reported that Hurley used a toothbrush to spatter paint on a part of his paintings. When he began to paint complete water colors in this manner, he called them "spattergraphs." Very often he used fish or birds as the main motifs in his designs; and he frequently would use the shapes of the flasks in the laboratory, or mathematical forms, particularly the triangle and the circle. (Plates V, VI, XVII, XVIII, XIX, XX).

"I am planning some spattergraphs as a change from the elevator theme," he wrote in his diary early in 1952. "I find it very exciting to build up a new design with stencils and cutouts—spraying colors through these. There is hardly any limit to its variations and creative possibilities."

A week later he noted, no doubt with a long sigh of regret, "I will have to stop spattergraphs and build up stock of saleable type." This was a recurring lament—"Sales brisk at lab, but I want to do something more creative"—"My serious work, which takes time and thought, seldom has a market."

The truth of it was, he had the time of his life creating his abstracts, for in them he was expressing his own personality, not, as in the landscapes, his response to external nature. His whimsy, his delight in harmonious design, the sense of rhythm that he felt in all creation—these were the qualities that he expressed in his abstracts. It is not insignificant that they appealed to Murray Adaskin, then head of the university's music department. Naturally, the abstracts had a more restricted appeal than the landscapes, for the latter aroused an associative as well as an esthetic response. By the 1950's regionalism had become a phase of the past and had been succeeded by exciting, and sometimes wild, experimentation on the part of most artists. Even the nationalism, which had developed during World War II as Canada's stature had grown, had merged with internationalism in the realm of art as Canadian artists traveled to world art centers to study and to soak in the modern theories which were exploding in a dozen different directions from abstract expressionism to automatism to the color-form compositions. In Saskatoon in the late 1940's George Swinton at the Art Centre and Nikola Bjelajac at the university, to mention only two, were stirring up interest in new art forms. Eva Mendel opened Bill Perehudoff's eyes to the magic of impressionism and prepared him emotionally to begin his wanderings—to Colorado to study under the world-famous muralist Jean Charlot, to the Ozenfant school in New York, and finally to Paris. In the early 1950's the university's art department had mapped out a greatly expanded program, which included intensive practical instruction. Eli Bornstein, another artist trained in Wisconsin, had followed Mr. Bjelajac. He was to gain international recognition as a structurist, and he was soon joined by other enthusiastic young instructors who were thoroughly up-to-date in their thinking and teaching methods. The stage was set for a virtual revolution in matters of art.

The stage extended from Saskatoon to Regina, where the chief performers were a group of young artists including Kenneth Lochhead, Arthur McKay, Ted Godwin, Ronald L. Bloore, and Douglas Morton (who became known for a time as the Regina Five), and a few years later, to the summer workshop at Emma Lake where the teachings of visiting New York artists, starting with Barnett Newman in 1959, had a tremendous impact on art in Saskatchewan. But all this is not part of the Hurley story.

In the midst of all the excitement Robert Hurley remained serenely and supremely himself. Not only was he not a part of it, but he was quite unsympathetic. When he went to the opening of a show of students' work, he found most of it pitiful, considering that it represented five months of instruction. "To paint a tree like a tree is regarded as old-fashioned," he remarked, adding "poor students—poor public." In the letter he wrote to the *Star-Phoenix* in 1955, he protested against "the hideous daubs inflicted on the helpless public." In a brief article that he wrote for *The Yorktoner* in 1958, he asked the question, "Is there a truly Saskatchewan art?" and he answered it with a decisive "No." He expressed regret that most artists and students were turning out "bizarre canvases and mediocre imitations of great modern painters," and he urged any artists resident in Saskatchewan "to go light on the cubistic or nondescript art and explore the wealth of Saskatchewan's landscape and people." Mr. Hurley was, indeed, a long way out of line.

His reference to "great modern painters," however, indicates that he was on familiar terms with the works of recognized masters. In 1938 when he was fascinated by the number of seeds in a sunflower head, he brought Van Gogh into his comments on the profusion of nature. "Van Gogh," he wrote, "wizard of the palette, eccentric and modernist, has immortalized the sunflower for us and undoubtedly reveled in the richness of chrome petal, as his strong yet excitable hands placed creamy pigment on canvas, in magical order." Hurley's own long-fingered hands, incidentally, are remarkably strong yet capable of the most delicate work.

Order and color were two qualities which Mr. Hurley valued highly. He experimented with color almost as much as with design, and many of his landscapes are as experimental as his abstracts for his use of color. One diary entry reads, ". . . went experimental, doing two sunset effects using strong contrasting purples, pink and lemon yellow sky area scrambled quickly with an old housepaint brush having rough texture—quite exciting." And again, ". . . played around with color and got down to doing two potboilers which I like for their simplicity and clean color. Both different color versions of the same theme—white snow—gray sky—yellow grass through the snow."

After browsing through some art books when he took a couple of paintings to James Art Studio for framing, he wrote: "Renoir is exquisite as a figure painter, but I can't stand Chagall (not surprising, considering Hurley's love of order.) Miro's stuff gives me the creeps, but I get a big laugh out of Paul Klee's fantastic 'stick-and-line' creations. I am experimenting along similar lines using automatic pen doodles to create patterns. Perhaps I can cut stencils and use in spattergraphs the most interesting of these doodles. It may be crazy—but it's good fun." He later changed his opinion about "Miro's stuff," finding a lot of humor in that artist's work and admiring his "tremendous facility for ideas."

Elaborating on his experimentation with pen doodles, he wrote: "Using a ballnib pen I concentrate on a mental design and let the pen trace the same on paper, with many amazingly good line patterns. I think much abstract art is just that. Perhaps I can originate a new art idiom—Doodlegraphic Art. I am studying Paul Klee and have a suspicion his amazing stick-and-line art is done by automatic doodling."

Hurley, by the way, didn't read about art, except for its broad history.

He owned a number of books about individual artists, such as Derain, Van Gogh, Gauguin, Utrillo, Lautrec, and Renoir, and he studied the reproductions in them; he also collected color reproductions from art journals. If critics, such as Terry Fenton in Regina, see the influence of the Bauhaus on Hurley, it is because of his study of Klee's work. He had never heard of the Bauhaus.

Hurley's experiments with automatic doodling and accidental designs resembled experiments that artists were making all over the Western world, but he wasn't aware of their experiments through reading about them. His approach to painting was entirely emotional and visual, not intellectual. Problems of esthetics he was content to leave to the thinkers and philosophers. He realized that thinking about them would likely result in confusing him and spoiling the directness of his approach. His attitude of remaining apart from current excitements probably accounted for the fact that he, unlike many artists, has no phases or periods dividing one type of work from another. He created abstracts at the same time that he painted landscapes; and his experiments with color coincided with his experiments with designs.

Though he didn't read about artists, he read about the fundamentals of design, just as he had read about the fundamentals of water-color painting. In 1952 he was busy studying G. J. Feldsted's *Design Fundamentals* (Sir Isaac Pitman & Sons (Canada) Ltd., Toronto, 1950), and *Composition, A Series of Exercises in Art Structure for the Use of Students and Teachers,* by Arthur W. Dow (Doubleday, Doran & Company, Inc., New York, 1938). He derived much benefit from them, he said, but noted with some satisfaction that he had been practicing most of the fundamentals intuitively, without understanding the principles behind them.

For his abstract paintings he experimented, too, with building designs partly from "found" materials, such as cloth, wire, string, papers of various textures, wooden slabs, mesh vegetable bags, leaves, and other odds and ends. He glued the materials to wood blocks and, using poster colors, stamped the designs on tinted show cards. As with the stencils, there was no end to the variety of designs or to the textural possibilities.

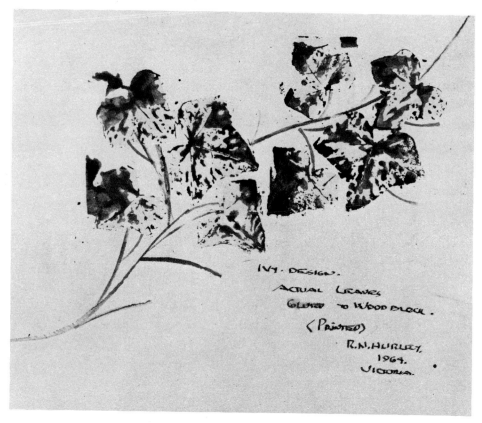

The artist was fascinated with design possibilities and was ingenious in the use he made of different materials. The chance designs resulting from taking prints from paint on glass always delighted him. (opposite page).

Another "trick" in which he delighted was to take a print from colors mixed on a pane of glass or a piece of cardboard. He found these handpressed prints, no two alike, to be especially effective for Christmas greeting cards. In 1956, he sold one customer a hundred of them for twenty-five cents each.

In his burrowing through the university library he came across a book that was somewhat of a curiosity, *An Illustrated Dictionary of Words Used in Art and Archaeology,* by J. W. Mollett, B.A., with the subtitle "Explaining Terms Frequently Used in Works on Architecture, Arms, Bronzes, Christian Art, Colour, Costume, Decoration, Devices, Emblems, Heraldry, Lace, Personal Ornaments, Pottery, Painting, Sculpture, etc., with their Derivations." It was published in London in 1883, and it is full of quaint and fascinating information. It contains 700 engravings, most of them small, intricate, and delicate, many of them illustrating symbolic birds, flowers, and beasts, and

M MUSIC.

HORN of METAL or OX-HORN

SYRINX. OR PANPIPES GEN.4.21

FLUTE DANIEL.3.5.

MARIMBA

1st. SAM. 18.46 SHALISHIM (TRIANGLE)

DRUM (TOPH.)

INVENTOR JUBAL GEN.4.21.

TIMBREL

PIPES

JOB.21.12 MENTION OF THE HARP — ORGAN PLEASURES OF THE UNGODLY.

LYRE (EGYPTIAN)

HARP

2.SAMUEL.6-5. SISTRUM. SISTRA (MENNA-O)

SISTRA 2.SAMUEL.6.5.

DAN.3.

THE DULCIMER

CYMBALS

R.N.HURLEY. 1996.

scores of them showing details of ornamental designs. Mr. Hurley certainly enriched his store of unusual facts from the *Illustrated Dictionary,* but more important for him, it gave him new ideas for an activity that was related to his art, to his religion, to his reading, and to his hobby of collecting.

For his own entertainment he composed illustrated alphabets based on his readings about natural history and travel. If he were reading about Australia, for instance, "A" would stand for "Adelaide" or "aborigine," "B" for "boomerang," and so on. He composed an "ABC" for Hooker's *Himalayan Journals,* and planned to draw a picture map of India.

He used the material he accumulated in this way as a basis for what he called his chalk talks, one of which, to the Apostolic Bible Institute in 1953, he described briefly in his diary: "In the limits of a two-hour lecture I could merely scratch the surface of the vast amount of the material I have in my mind. My first idea was to show them how to illustrate a spiritual truth. I took the idea of Hell or the Bottomless Pit (Abyss)—graphically showing with a few simple strokes people falling down an awful chasm. I then took the theme Bread of Life, reading a suitable scripture, and illustrated it with a landscape of a Western harvest scene." And he found scriptural texts to go with musical instruments for "M."

The little figures dancing around the illustrations for "M" were inspired when he was eating macaroni, "the curved pieces sparking the idea." From time to time he worked out several macaroni-inspired doodles and created various groups of men in action "such as aboriginals doing a war dance, groups of Indians skirmishing, acrobats, dancers, natives attacking a dinosaur. These macaroni men," he wrote, "can be arranged into all sorts of designs." And through them, he could certainly give rein to his sense of fun.

He spent a fair amount of time at the lab blackboard, when things were quiet, drawing "simple objects with a view to developing more freedom in drawing and experimenting in design.. . . I find it very stimulating as it forces me to study carefully the basic forms, such as the double triangle of a goldfish, crab based on a circle, bird shaped on a variation of an oval, etc."

Also, he copied several Asiatic scripts "as a training for the hand and eye. It is very intriguing to draw the queer characters of say the Tigrinya (Abyssinia), Lapaki (India). Burmese is a geometric script based on a circle while Bugis from Celebes is based on a triangle." He copied the scripts from a tiny book (about two by three inches) he purchased from the British Foreign Bible Society who circulated it as an aid for translating the Bible. A "nice quality handglass for reading purposes" which he received, along with a Mozart record, for his birthday in 1952 from Loren Teed, Norman Caplin, and Eli Bornstein, must have come in mighty handy!

A page from one of Hurley's illustrated alphabets. He illustrated many of the talks he gave by drawing similar objects as these with chalk on a blackboard.   India ink and crayon

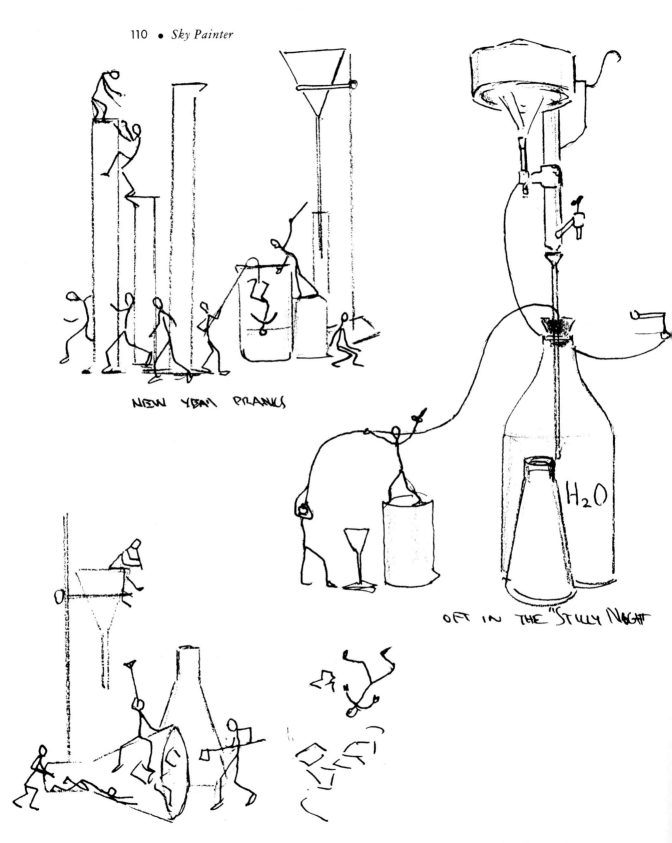

NEW YEAR PRANKS

OFT IN THE "STILLY NIGHT

H_2O

His macaroni men indulge in pranks, allowing the artist to give free rein to the whimsical side of his nature.

India ink and pencil

As he continued to build up his repertoire of chalk-talk material, he found that "this sketching from detailed cuts disciplines the mind and eye." The sketches reproduced here are from ones retained in his private collection.

Speaking of collections, Mr. Hurley had what he called a "mania" for collecting. "Adding to my ever-growing stack of stamps and reproductions of fine art, I've started slashing with a razor blade all the old magazines I get my hands on in quest of trade-marks and commercial art with which I hope to compile a scrapbook for future use. It is very exciting as well as stimulating to delve often into such a store of art designs." Once, when leafing through his scrapbooks, he got a sudden inspiration for his Christmas card, and noted, "This is where my storehouse of cuts and prints comes in useful." In addition to periodicals with fine color reproductions, he cut out advertisements from the *Star-Phoenix* and filed them away alphabetically for possible re-creation in his stick-print technique.

When he was feeling too tired to paint or to draw designs, he would refresh his ideas by going through his clippings, for he had what he considered "a really priceless collection of color cuts and black-and-whites all pasted methodically in dozens of albums and scrapbooks listed under subjects."

When the Russians sent their first sputnik into orbit in 1957, Hurley coined the name "Hurleynick" for his abstract paintings. Compared to his landscapes they were artificial in the sense that they were not based on the realities of external nature but were composed solely by his imagination, an imagination fed by his wide reading, his studies of paintings and designs, and his sense of the harmony and rhythm of the universe as the work of a Great Designer.

The world of the imagination was as real to Hurley as were the sunsets and grain elevators and telephone poles that he painted for the public. He was reported in an interview in 1958 as saying that he was having the time of his life experimenting with new techniques for achieving unusual effects in his abstracts. Called by any name, they all reflect his sense of fun, his whimsy, his sheer creative joy. In them, the frustrated musician in Hurley was released.

Lack of time was his enemy as far as his abstract painting was concerned. The real world kept intruding with its demands on his talents and with just the business of living and making a living.

An example of the artist's preoccupation with designs

India ink

12

"Forward till Upward"

AN EVANGELICAL MISSIONARY was asked once, after a six-year tour, "What next?" His reply was, "Forward till Upward!" If Mr. Hurley had been asked the same question after the presentation of his paintings to Royalty in 1951, his answer would have been the same, and he would have meant it in the same way. The phrase "forward till upward," however, was to have an added meaning for him before the decade was over, a meaning he wouldn't in his wildest imaginings have dreamed possible. He described the presentation of his water colors to Important Persons and the hearing of his voice over the radio when interviewed by Dan Worden as "thrills." There were more "thrills" in store for him during what were to be the most decisive years of his life, between the ages of fifty-eight and sixty-eight.

The first thrill came in 1952 during the celebrations on the occasion of Saskatoon's seventieth birthday, not as a city but as a place on a map. It had been in 1882 that John Lake, first commissioner of the Temperance Colonization Society, had stood on the high banks of the South Saskatchewan River and uttered the historic words: "Arise, Saskatoon, Queen of the North." In August, 1952, Hurley was the honored guest at a noonday ceremony and luncheon sponsored by the Kiwanis Club, and was introduced by A. M. Blue as a man who had made an outstanding contribution to the life of Saskatoon.

He was to be honored twice by the prairie city; on December the tenth, 1962, when Mayor Sidney L. Buckwold presented him with an Award of Merit from the city of Saskatoon prior to his departure from the Prairies, and on May the twenty-sixth, 1966, on the occasion of the city's sixtieth birthday when he received a letter from Carl McLeod, the assistant city commissioner, conveying the thanks and appreciation of the citizens of Saskatoon for his contribution to the community, accompanied by a plaque signed by Mayor Ernest Cole.

Not only did the demand for his landscapes increase as he became more celebrated—one can only imagine the number of Kiwanians who wanted Hurleys after the noonday happening, especially when Kiwanian Bill Moore who had once headed Saskatoon's YMCA could fill them in on Hurley's poverty-stricken days at the "Y" as a young English immigrant—but the demands for personal appearances increased too. He gave water-color demonstrations to school classes, church groups, the Fortnightly Club, the Quota Club, the University Women's Club, the Canadian Women's Press Club, the Art Centre, and to a point where he remarked "Saskatoon is a well-clubbed city!" He was a little nervous about giving a demonstration to the Newman Club at St. Thomas More College, for Catholicism was out-of-bounds in his religion, and his nervousness was increased when his braces broke as he was gathering up his materials in the lab; but the professor who had asked him to demonstrate put him at his ease, and he found the students among the most receptive of any audience he had had. At one demonstration, when he was so weary that the work was an effort, he painted a water color in twenty-three minutes.

He always donated the water colors to the groups, and they would be raffled or auctioned, with the monies going to the usual good causes. The liveliest auction on record was conducted by the Blacklock Brothers, agricultural auctioneers, in 1958 at a dinner of the Saskatchewan Agricultural Graduates' Association. The graduates had bought eight Hurleys at the going rate of ten, fifteen, or twenty dollars each. Jock, Benny, and Bill Blacklock went into action, with Ken Gronsdahl as the bid-taker, and the association realized a healthy profit. The press report ended in this fashion: "And modest Mr. Hurley drew the biggest hand of all. He was applauded with more vigor than they ever heard at a Calgary bull sale."

And the sketching trips continued, sometimes for sheer pleasure, sometimes for the sheer necessity of replenishing his stock of landscape notes. When he went alone he would walk around Sutherland, or go as far as the open prairie a half mile east of the town, or, occasionally, hike as far as Sutherland Beach; or he would take a bus to the Exhibition Grounds and walk west to the river, or to the opposite side of the river as far as the Arctic Ice Company plant and sketch the rocks and sandbars leading south to the G. T. P. Bridge and Yorath Island.

Frequently he went off by car with his old friend Mr. Wickenden—to Cranberry Flats, Beaver Creek, Pike Lake and Barnes Lake (Plate XXIII), a little lake near Pike Lake which they had discovered and liked for its solitude and pictorial allurements—"a marshy sanctuary for wild fowl, beaver and deer,"—or to a rocky ridge about sixteen miles east of Sutherland, where the ladies would accompany them in the late summer to pick berries, or to Clark's Crossing, where the fishing was good.

Early in the fifties, Hurley sat for Mr. Wickenden, and the portrait, in pastels, is one of Isabella's hoarded treasures. Friends would drop in after the portrait-sitting sessions and the talk would go on until the small hours about God and man and the world from very divergent viewpoints but always amicably offered.

Then there were the longer sketching trips when he accompanied the scientists at the lab. He wrote a description of one such trip, which stands as a good model for most of them:

"Tried a sketch of a lone red elevator perched on a boulder-strewn ridge. Creek water a lovely pale blue snaking both sides of highway into Moose Jaw. Refueled in the city; then north for Buffalo Pound Lake which we made for the midday meal overlooking a fine panorama. Dinner of spam and toast made on the embers of chokecherry fire. Sun very hot again at 1:30 p.m. which added to the discomfort of cockleburs and stinging nettles and the ever-persistent mosquitoes. Saw some spectacular masses of pink wild bergamot and golden rod. Some mallards cruising on Buffalo

Mr. Wickenden's portrait of Hurley, one of the treasures Isabella keeps in her metal trunk ▶
pastel

Lake. Across lake by a bridge and winding road. Very scenic but unable to pencilograph owing to winding road spoiling chances for at least a one-minute sketch. Jotted down notes on vegetation; sky formations, shacks, willow bluffs, sloughs, etc. Erosion in coulee.

"North from Buffalo Park to Chamberlain. The twisting highway trailing up and across two more coulee troughs until we reached the main drag. Party stopped for crop surveys—while I did some notes of a rock pile at the corner mark of a section of freshly worked summer fallow. Farm a half mile south. Strip of ochre where wheat is ripening. Nearing Tuxford, road allowances rich with helianthus—golden yellow. This with the blue graded sky and dark green of willows made a pleasing color scheme. Near town of Holdfast got a graph dashing through a gravel cut with telephone poles tapering off to Penzance elevators. Forty miles per hour through Liberty, Stalwart, Imperial, etc., taking fast shots with prismacolor noting road color, herbage, boulders, silo, cowbarns. Some crows holding convention over rabbit carcass, result of a traffic mishap. Nice stands of barley, wheat alternating with lilac aster, fireweed, and golden rod. Surveying crops every ten miles. Owing to hot blast of last week, much of the grain will be lucky to make three bushels per acre.

"On through Simpson to Watrous where we made evening meal near lake shore. Was disappointed at not being able to capture in water color the blue of Lake Manitou owing to a stiff breeze stirring up a surf of whitecaps. Now quite chilly, so made a jolly coffee boil over brush fire. Saw a few bathing beauties shivering on the way back from the turbulent lake. Home via Young, Elstow, Blucher, and Floral, doing a spectacular sunset in gold and purples (Plate XIV) which I worked up later in water colors. Home at 9:30 with a big sheaf of notes, scrawls and scribbles to be used as source material for future paintings."

Nothing much escaped the artist's eye!

Hurley often made shorter excursions with Dr. Russell to sketch scenes which could be used as the basis of illustrations for the material which Dr. Russell had collected on the Carlton Trail, an old road which had played an important part in the story of the opening of the West as travelers had followed it from Portage Avenue in Winnipeg past Portage la Prairie and Fort Ellice, through the Touchwood Hills, southeast of Saskatoon, and on to Fort Carlton, crossing the South Saskatchewan River at Batoche. As a guest at the Russell home for lunch or tea he would pore through the collection of priceless old photographs depicting life on the trail and read the descriptions of it. Dr. Russell also drove him to the Western Development Museum in Saskatoon to check on details at firsthand.

When episodes about the Carlton Trail were published in *The Western Producer* in 1956, the year after its publication in book form, they were illustrated with reproductions of Hurley paintings which featured carts and camps and people in the foreground. As models for the figure drawings, Mr. Hurley called on the services of friends and relatives.

Dr. Russell had a second hobby—the identification of Saskatchewan weeds and native plants. While Hurley sketched, Dr. Russell would collect plants.

Often, if the weather were not favorable for sketching, Hurley would help with the collecting. After such "sketching" trips, his diary entries would read: ". . . spread out botanical collections to dry," "pressed specimens," "at work pressing herbarium specimens for botanical collection," "have started mounting RCR's 1952 collection of herbarium material—sedges, grasses, shrubs, and weeds." Mr. Hurley, with his gardening experience and his love of nature, shared Dr. Russell's interest in the native plants, and his trained powers of observation aided him in spotting unusual specimens. He mounted a small private collection, which he used as inspiration for designs.

Young Bob Hurley had left London jobs to go to work on farms because he liked the outdoors; artist Robert Hurley got a cooped-up feeling when he had to spend long stretches in the laboratory, and the sketching trips brought wonderful relief. Once, in the early summer when the lab work was of a particularly demanding nature, he wrote, with a touch of wistfulness, "I would like to devote all summer and fall to a closer study of nature which is really the great source of art inspiration." Often, when he was at a low ebb physically, he would toy with the idea of asking for a few days' leave of absence. Occasionally he followed up the idea, and the diary reader doesn't find him resting in his armchair or relaxing in the sun but rather going by car to Yorath Island and Patience Lake, or taking the bus to the end of the exhibition line or to re-explore the Nutana heights where he had worked as a gardener, crossing the C.N. bridge (now part of Saskatoon's freeway) on foot to make another sketch of the familiar old power house close to the old Technical Collegiate. And the trips always revived him, even though they didn't cure his anemia or eczema.

Yet, when he was on an extended and enforced leave of absence owing to poor health, he was impatient to get back to the lab. Apparently, the old town-versus-country conflict still pulsed in him.

Perhaps the most sentimental of sketching trips he made during the 1950's were those he took by himself back to "The Magic Mile." These were made easy after the Hurleys' daughter Alice married and moved to her own home on Empress Street in the North Park district of Saskatoon, within walking distance of Goldeye Bay where the river bends from east to north. Alice had married Alvin Funk, the son of John Funk who years before had exhibited in the same shows as Hurley at the Exhibition and who had since moved his family East. Alvin had returned to Saskatoon after World War II.

There was much visiting between the Hurleys and the Funks, with mentions of roast goose at New Year's, duck at Thanksgiving, goldeyes topped off with rhubarb pie and ice cream on Saturday nights, making their mouth-watering appearance in the diary. After John Alexander was born, the grandparents would sometimes take over on Saturdays as baby sitters, and Robert, equipped with sketching materials, would make his happy way to Goldeye Bay. With Chuck living at home, after a stint of work in Calgary, and "little Jackie" joining the Funks, the family get-togethers were happy occasions.

The diary contains frequent references, too, to gatherings of friends at the Hurley home, especially after Dr. Ledingham started to take photographs of Hurley water colors before they were snapped up by the public. The Saskatoon Camera Club had been one of the founding societies of the Art Centre, and there had always been mutual interest between the two classes of artists. When Hurley's interest in photography was aroused, photographers and artists were often invited for a color-slide party, with Jim Hogg of the Camera Club operating his projector until the Hurleys invested in one and learned how to use. it.

To his chalk talks and his water color demonstrations, Mr. Hurley added talks accompanied by slides as he became increasingly absorbed in what the eye of the camera could select from a scene.

Another project which interested him for a couple of summers was conducting a sketching class. Mr. Hurley's first pupil had been Rev. Percy Hicks, who had come upon him while he was painting the Sutherland elevator and had asked permission to watch. Hurley agreed, and began to show him the basics then and there. The lessons continued for some time and even after Mr. Hicks moved to Ontario, he would send paintings to his teacher for comment. Hurley's sketching class was a small one, but although he enjoyed being with students eager to learn, he found it too demanding of his time. He was always willing to help, however, if anyone asked for advice, remembering how he had valued encouragement in the thirties.

His life followed a fairly regular pattern, alternating between work at the lab with the welcome sketching trips during the forst-free months, and painting at home with time out for gardening and entertaining. Sundays he reserved for church, reading, and music. He had bought a record player, and began collecting works by his favorite composers. When the radio offered nothing but "Hollywood garbage," he would treat himself to a record concert.

His visits to the Art Centre became less frequent as the pressure of filling the demand for his landscapes became greater. His natural aversion to frivolity and idle chatter made it easy for him to refuse social invitations except to the homes of close and valued friends and relatives. The wonder was, not that he stayed as close to home as he did, but that he found time to give his talks and demonstrations, for he seldom had a large enough supply of paintings on hand to fill the requests for them.

In the spring of 1956 he felt "rotten and tired" all the time, and their Sutherland physician, who was treating Isabella for quinsy in May, decided he should have a tuberculin test. The test was negative, but the cough and soreness in the chest persisted. Even being anointed with oil at the altar didn't bring the "sweet release" for which he had hoped.

Sales at the lab continued so brisk that it became a day-by-day effort to produce sufficient paintings. Whatever else art may be, it shouldn't have much connection with mass production. Ailing Mr. Hurley became so depressed and frustrated by lack of time that he considered retiring from his work. He talked matters over with Dr. Simmonds, who persuaded him to stay on but to take some of his vacation time to rest and to paint.

On June the eleventh he started a one-week vacation, and planned to finish two paintings daily. One day he went for a car trip to the television tower east of Sutherland to sketch, and the next day he went to Clark's Crossing with G. A. Batke, his pastor at the Apostolic Church, and received encouragement and strength through conversing with him. The following day he was able to work up several cloud studies on Bristol board, a fine, smooth pasteboard which he usually avoided as being difficult to use, but which was good for atmospheric effects. Once before, when trying to catch up on paintings for sale, he noted, "I flopped on two quickies because I used smooth mat board—which doesn't work as well as pebble." With few exceptions, all of Mr. Hurley's paintings have been on pebble board, or duplex board. In 1951, he recorded buying enough pebble board at James Art Studio "ot last for a year." In 1972, he reported, "I prefer it to conventional paper, as one does not have to waste valuable time to stretch it."

He went back to work, but change of a different sort was in the air. In mid-July the Hurleys sold their home on Railway Avenue for $3,800 cash, about five times as much as they had paid for it, but they had made considerable improvements during their fourteen years of residence. Mr. Hurley entertained the thought of collecting their assets, taking a trip to Britain, and sketching along the Thames, but the idea was vetoed, probably by Mrs. Hurley, who had become a victim of rheumatoid arthritis. At any rate, they decided to buy a new and roomy house located at 418 111th Street, Sutherland, a decision they were happy to have made when Alice and their grandson lived with them for several months while Alvin completed the work for his doctor's degree in forestry at the University of Toronto.

In August of 1956 Hurley left by train for Vancouver to visit with Stan Brunst. He enjoyed the face-to-face continuation of their long friendship and the respite from work, but found it difficult to keep up with the driving energy of Brunst as they hustled and bustled from one interesting place to another, with pauses only to sketch when a particular scene caught their fancy. They had a rare time together, which became doubly precious in memory when Hurley received the news of Brunst's death two years later. Hurley returned feeling more able to cope with the problem of lack of time.

However, a rumor that he heard in the late fall added fuel to the fire of Hurley's desire to do nothing but paint. "I hear there is a conspiracy underway," he wrote, "to persuade the CCF Government to turn me loose to paint our Beautiful Saskatchewan with good salary (I hope)."

He heard nothing more, apparently, for in the spring of 1958, shortly after his sixty-fourth birthday, he was busy soliciting letters of recommendation to back his application for a grant from the Canada Council. And the letters came pouring back. It must be doubtful if any application had ever been more enthusiastically supported, to the tune of a score of letters.

Premier T. C. Douglas wrote:

"I have known Mr. Hurley for quite a number of years now and I am the proud owner of some of his water colors. I think Mr. Hurley has great talent in portraying prairie scenes and his paintings have had a wide appeal for prairie people who live elsewhere on this continent and abroad. Our Agent General in London tells me that he receives many requests from Saskatchewan people living overseas for Mr. Hurley's paintings because they are so reminiscent of their home province."

Dr. P. M. Simmonds, "the chief," wrote that "he is a very capable worker, very humble and sincere."

Dr. J. W. T. Spinks, then dean of graduate studies at the university, wrote:

"Mr. Hurley is a modest and unassuming man who has developed a very considerable skill as a painter in water colors."

Eric Knowles, editor of the *Star-Phoenix,* wrote:

"Robert Hurley has likely done more than any other person to bring Saskatchewan art to the attention of the general Canadian public."

Dr. Max Stern, of the Dominion Gallery of Fine Arts, Montreal, wrote:

"I found Hurley's work artistically as well as documentally the finest representation of the Prairie landscape."

Dr. J. B. Mawdsley, head of the university's department of geology and president of the Saskatoon Art Centre in its early years, wrote:

"Hurley is the one who has best caught the subtle and elusive quality of our scenery and the breadth of our skies."

So the letters went, all praising his skill, all commenting on his ability to paint the prairie landscape.

Stanley Obodiac, who had come to know Hurley well when he was writing about him, wrote to him, saying, "your latest art successes have me in joy," and predicting that Mr. Hurley would get a grant, for, after all, hadn't Ken Lochhead been granted thousands of dollars to paint a mural in the airport at Gander?

Hurley was informed by the Canada Council, however, that his application had been filed too late for any monies to be granted to him that year. The glowing and ready letters of recommendation went a long way to easing the disappointment.

On Easter Sunday he attended the service in the Salvation Army Citadel, and then, on a drive to Pike Lake, he "got a real thrill" passing the new power house of the SPC, for he had just received a commission to do a painting of it for Queen Elizabeth.

In May, he was receiving letters of recommendation with regard to being granted an art retainer by the Government of Saskatchewan; and shortly after his painting had been presented to the Queen in July, he received news that the Government had granted the art retainer.

The Honorable Mr. Sturdy, assistant to the premier, in announcing the retainership in August, said: "We recognize the skill of Bob Hurley as an artist. It is my opinion that he portrays the Saskatchewan scene more graphically than any Saskatchewan artist has attempted to do in the past. We would like to see him given an opportunity to exploit his talents, and feel that his best work lies ahead of him."

The retainer was for $2,000 a year. It was stated in the press account of the retainer that the government would also purchase thirty paintings at the rate of fifty dollars each for the first ten, thirty-five dollars each for the next ten, and twenty-five each for the remainder. However, this proposal was not written into any agreement, and a search through government records reveals that the artist, during the three years of the retainership, was commissioned to paint twenty water colors. As there is no record of his having been paid for them, they were likely a condition which was attached to the $2,000 grant. The paintings are still in various government offices in Regina.

The establishment of a retainership for an artist was a "first" in the history of Saskatchewan—and likely a "first" for any province. More than any other recognition that could have come his way, recognition by the province that he had helped to put on the map of the world through his painting was the highest honor.

He didn't record his "thrill" but he did say, "Life begins at sixty-five, not at forty!" One of his first acts was to buy a camera so that he could build up a supply of color slides to add to his store of sketches and pencil notes. He would paint the province as he had never painted it before!

Mr. Hurley retired from his work at the laboratory where he had spent sixteen crowded and productive years, aided and abetted by the plant pathologists as tenderly as they cared for their botanical specimens. They gave him a fitting send-off, even to the presentation by The Chief of the first Hurley painting he had bought. It wasn't a complete break, for the men at the lab were not only fellow workers, they were friends.

The news of the art retainer brought reporters to the door of 418 to find out what the painter laureate of Saskatchewan planned to do with his new-found, wonderful time. Idabelle Melville, for the *Star-Phoenix,*

Dr. R. J. Ledingham
At the lab, shortly before his retirement, 1958

found him in his workroom, happy and relaxed, experimenting further with the technique he had devised in 1955 which involved the use of "found" material, and he gave her a demonstration of the variety of designs and of textural effects he could achieve. He called the paintings "monoprints" and thought them "the most creative work I have ever done."

The demand for Hurley landscapes continued, and not being pressed for time, he was able to keep a few jumps ahead of his admiring pursuers, working even more meticulously than he had when he had started painting again after his 1955 hospital confinement. He added to his stock of sketches, refreshed old ones, and used the lessons he was learning through his experimental work to bring his landscapes nearer to a pure distillation of the Prairies.

Glimpses of him at home reveal him indulging in his musical pastimes, shaking the bones, and tapping out airs on the glassware. In a letter in his collection from Mrs. Sills, of Edmonton, she refers to the success of one of their homemade concerts which she had taped when visiting him. He often enjoyed work-outs on his guitar, but regretted that store teeth prevented him from playing his harmonicas. While walking near home one day he expressed this regret to an old railroader he met who was playing a harmonica in chorus with the birds. "Oh," said the old man, "I just take my teeth out and blow like Hell!" Hurley intends to try this yet.

Wherever he went he took his camera, and it was with him when he and Isabella drove with Chuck to the West Coast in August, 1959, for Chuck's marriage to Elaine Bailey, of Haney, British Columbia. After the wedding, the Hurleys spent a week on Vancouver Island, where Alice and Alvin had settled.

On September the third, homeward bound, Robert and Isabella boarded a Trans Canada Airlines plane at Vancouver, rather against a nervous Robert's wishes. They were barely air-borne, however, before he was enthralled by the sensation. Out came the camera. To his dismay, he had only a few shots left, but the photographs that might have been, stayed in his mind to tease and nag at him until he found a way of getting aloft again.

Hurley had been fascinated when Dr. Ansten Anstensen, head of the university's department of Germanic languages, had described the magnificence of the Spanish countryside as seen from a plane, but it wasn't until he experienced the marvels of aerial vision for himself that he fully realized the possibilities for water-color painting.

September the third was a red-letter date in Hurley's life. It was perhaps only natural that the man who had painted the skies should love the sensation of being a very part of the clouds he so much admired from the ground. And looking down, he saw the patterns and rhythms of the landscape as he had never imagined them to be when he painted them from ground level. He was impatient to fly again, and he made arrangements with Pacific Western Airlines at the Saskatoon airport to travel as a photographer-passenger whenever the weather was fine.

Upward and upward and upward! Mr. Hurley made twenty-five flights in all, most of them on D.C. 3's. The pilots got to know him well and adjusted their flying to permit him to snap the scenes he most wanted, and he took scores of photographs. Constantly he was amazed as he saw familiar territory from a new perspective—the lumber country north of Prince Albert, the wild terrain around Eagle Hills, the sandhills of Dundurn, the huge farms on the Regina plains, and the winding courses of the Saskatchewan rivers. He made two flights over the Rockies, attempting to record the changes from prairie to rangeland, from foothills to awesome peaks.

In his workroom he built tiny cardboard models of farm buildings, and miniature corrals and fences, painted them appropriate colors, and set them up wherever there was floor space available in the house to use as references when he was designing an aerial landscape.

A new type of patron appeared at the Hurley door—the airmen. They came at first out of curiosity to see what the artist was making from his photographs; they remained out of interest; and they usually left with a water color in their hands and their pockets lighter by the usual fifteen, twenty, or twenty-five-dollar charge. And, of course, as the paintings got back to the airport, friends and families and associates of the airmen drove over to 418.

When the Federal Government decided to close the Royal Canadian Air Force base at Saskatoon in the early 1960's, the clamor by the men for

Hurley aerial paintings as treasured mementos of their prairie posting became so great that he was fortunate to be able to fill the request from Air Vice-Marshall H. M. Carscallen, of Ottawa. The painting reproduced here is from Dr. Anstensen's collection, a gift from a grateful "aerialist" (Plate XXVII).

The Government of Saskatchewan renewed the art retainer in August, 1960, for the third and last time, and he was to complete the twenty paintings which had been commissioned. The offices and public rooms in the Legislative Buildings in Regina became a small Hurley gallery. In Mr. Hurley's scrapbook is a clipping from the *Leader-Post* reporting the desire of Ross Thatcher for some Hurleys in the office of the leader of the opposition. He was tired, Mr. Thatcher was reported as saying, of looking only at pictures of Sir Wilfrid Laurier and the Rt. Hon. Mackenzie King, no doubt inherited from his predecessors in the office, and of his own fine, but not particularly esthetic, Hereford cattle. The item doesn't reveal if his desire was met—it likely was—but when he became premier in 1964, he probably had his pick of the pictures.

In the spring of 1961, Mr. Hurley again applied for a Canada Council grant, and again he had a battery of letters of recommendation, and again he was not successful on the grounds of having no particular project in mind. It was a reasonable rejection, as he was sixty-seven and there were many young artists who had definite goals in mind and who needed financial encouragement.

One of the pleasures of Mr. Hurley's life was the writing of illustrated letters (Plate XII). From his early days in Canada he had sent sketches back to England. Much later he developed a style of blending pictures and text—"pictographs," he called them. With Chuck and his wife living in Regina, and the Funks settled in Victoria, he had good scope for his whimsical missives. "The Tumbleweed Gazette," he called one series; the "Screwball Journal," another. At last the mixture of irrepressible Cockney and happy-go-lucky Irish could be given full play, for there were no insecurities, no obligations, no pressures to block its free expression. It had been a lonely, long, rough road, but the rainbow he had glimpsed and followed had proved to be no will-o'-the-wisp. It had led him to the pot of golden happiness.

The next decision, like so many since he had first met his Irish colleen in 1932, was Isabella-inspired. She missed her family, and she suffered from arthritis. The doctor recommended a milder climate. The answer was obvious. The Hurleys would move to Victoria. Bob, who had been Born Again in Saskatchewan, who had become its scenic spokesman, was reluctant to move. But health and heartstrings won the debate, and in late 1962, the Hurleys prepared to travel west.

13

To the Lighthouse

ONCE THE DECISION TO MOVE to Victoria was made there was no time for looking backward. The Hurleys had to make arrangements to dispose of their house, take stock of their financial position, and determine which of their possessions to take along. Once the decision to move was known to the public there was no need to wonder about what to do with any paintings Robert had on hand. He sold them all, salvaging only his precious stock of sketches and pencil notes so that he could use them as references when he could no longer see the prairie sky and the grain elevators reflected in the sloughs.

There were two memorable evenings, one private, when friends and neighbors gathered at the Hurley home with good wishes and regretful farewells, and one public, when a Hurley night was sponsored by the board of directors of the Saskatoon Art Centre on November the thirtieth. As the Art Centre was operating in makeshift quarters, arrangements were made to hold the event at the J. S. Wood branch of the Public Library—certainly a most appropriate location to honor an artist who honored Mr. Wood as one of his earliest and most encouraging supporters.

The auditorium was hung with Hurley paintings, some of which he hadn't seen for a score of years. They had been borrowed for the occasion from private collections, particularly those of Mrs. Caldwell and R. G. Doig, a retired bank manager who had collected Hurleys when he had served on the Art Centre board.

Surrounded by his own art, and introduced by his good companion of sketching days, Mr. Wickenden, Hurley took the stage, reminiscing about his Saskatchewan experiences and showing some of his many color slides. He was presented with a purse of money to ease the parting and a guest book signed by all who filled the hall. Among the well-wishing telegrams was one from Rt. Hon. John G. Diefenbaker, of Prince Albert, who was then the Prime Minister of Canada.

Bob and Isabella spent the Christmas season with Chuck and his family in Regina and were guests of honor at another Hurley night, sponsored by one of his chief patrons, the Government of Saskatchewan, and presided over by Premier Lloyd. Thus feted by his city and his province, Mr. Hurley left his Prairies with memories that would glow for many years.

In Victoria they stayed with the Funks, who helped with operation house-hunting. Before long they were "at home" again at 445 Walter Avenue, a street out of the stream of traffic in a quiet residential district in Saanich,

Bob and Isabella "at home" in Victoria

now part of Greater Victoria just as Sutherland is now part of Saskatoon. Their home is a short block away from hourly bus service to the center of the city and within walking distance of the Gorge, a long arm of the Pacific Ocean, where the city planners have reserved reasonable stretches of land for public parks. At the Tillicum end of their avenue, about ten minutes away on foot, is a fish and chips shop, reminding Bob of London town, and a doctors' office building, now decorated with two prairie land-scapes.

One of his first callers was Vivienne Chadwick, a feature writer for a Victoria newspaper. Her article was published in *The Islander* on March the twenty-fourth, 1963, under the title "Will Neptune Capture Robert Hurley, Prairie Painter?" Her opinion was that the sea would have an irresistible painting appeal for the artist, for it was, like the prairie, boundless.

He took his camera and sketch pad whenever he went on excursions to beauty spots around the city and the island, but he relied more on the camera than on his sketches to refresh his memory of scenes and colors which had caught his attention, for he had trained his eye to use color slides as the basis for paintings when he had taken his aerial shots. His camera became his substitute for the sketching companions and field trips of Saskatchewan days.

One view of the ocean which appealed to him very much because of its design and color-composition possibilities included the Fisgard Lighthouse off the naval base at Esquimalt Harbor (Plate XXVIII). It had much the same sort of quality as a prairie vista, with the lighthouse, like the elevator, standing as a symbol of man's relationship to the landscape. James M. Minifie, whom Mr. Hurley had met in 1957 during one of Mr. Minifie's speaking tours across Canada when he was the Washington correspondent for the CBC, and who had hung some Hurley landscapes in the American capital, was another visitor to the Hurley home in Victoria, and it was a painting of the lighthouse that he carried away with him to hang in his Victoria home.

In the spring of 1972, recalling the visit of the Minifies, Mr. Hurley's countenance softened with pleasure as he remarked that the most wonderful thing that had happened to him through his art had been to know the kindness of people, hundreds of people. And this, after he had been reliving, for the purposes of his biography, all the "thrills" that had come his way.

Even if Neptune had captured Mr. Hurley, he would not have had much opportunity to pay homage to the sea, for he was besieged with requests for his prairie paintings. People on the Prairies who had wanted Hurley paintings when they had heard that he was leaving (or that he had left) learned of his Victoria address from the letters he sent back and kept his postman busy delivering their requests. One of Isabella's cousins, Mrs. Milton Gould, had agreed to act as his Saskatoon agent for a while, and once that word got around, she had to keep after him to keep her supplied.

"If my paintings are potboilers," he said once, jokingly, "Mr. and Mrs. John Public certainly like my brand of soup." Dan Worden had quipped, when they were taping their interview, "What's wrong with making soup, as long as it's Good Soup."

Speaking of soup, he had recommended it as a cure-all in one of his "jingles," with the P.S., "No charge, Sir Thomas."

If you are allergic to ills problematic,
Bunions, Shingles, or Croup,
Quit your doubting, moaning, or pouting,
Go on a course (of course) of Lipton's soup.

It's a cinch that Hurley's "potboilers" are a pretty good tonic for an ailment known as homesickness, one commonly suffered by exiles from the Prairies, particularly if they can't see enough sky.

A distinguished visitor, Rt. Hon. J. G. Diefenbaker, at the Hurley home, April, 1971

One of the more recent prairie-bred visitors to make his way to Hurley's home was Mr. Diefenbaker in April of 1971, shortly after Bob's seventy-seventh birthday, and he, too, carried away a part of Saskatchewan, after being entertained by Mr. Hurley with the bones and the metal corset staves.

Meanwhile, back on the Prairies, on the campus where he had been a familiar figure for sixteeen years as he went on his errands from the lab to the Physics Building to the post office and to the university cafeteria for bacon rind bait, a scheme was developing to bring Mr. Hurley home. Not in person, for no one would have wished to expose him to the rigors of the Saskatchewan climate which had been mainly responsible for his decision to move away.

On March the eighth, 1966, Dr. Anstensen wrote to Mr. Hurley suggesting that he consider gathering material for the basis of a "Hurley collection" to be housed at the University of Saskatchewan. Hurley responded to the idea and to the letter with enthusiasm, and by April Dr. Anstensen was able to report that "regarding my proposal for the 'Hurleyana' collection, I can tell you it has been received very sympathetically by the University Administration and by the Departments of Geography and Geology, both of which have a definite interest in seeing your slides."

At the head of the university administration was President Spinks, the Dr. Spinks who had bought a little painting of wild roses more than thirty years before and who had continued to add to his private collection. After consultations with various departments, it was decided that the most suitable location for the collection was the Shortt Library of Canadiana.

By mid-April arrangements were fairly well consolidated and Mr. Hurley began to organize his material. In May, he sent some parcels off to Dr. Anstensen—"a few color notes, or pencil sketches, relative to my early efforts in teaching myself skills at drawing from real objects." He also sent a great many slides, including pictures of paintings, aerial shots, scenic pictures, and family shots. In June, in correspondence with D. C. Appelt, the university librarian, he announced that he was sending some more material and preparing more. In July, he reported to Dr. Anstensen that he still had a lot of photos and pencil sketches to forward, also his diary, part of which had been typed by Miss Ellard at the lab and part of which he was editing, as much of it was "trivial or poorly composed."

The original diaries and the edited diaries are both included in the collection, and of the two the original ones are the more interesting because they contain impressions at the time they were written. In the edited ones, he has changed emphasis and facts to make them sound better according to his way of thinking, but at times his altered facts don't jibe with real facts. In July, he wrote to Dr. Anstensen thanking him for being the "architect" of the Hurleyana idea.

During most of 1966, from March on, he worked at gathering and preparing material for the collection. He started writing his memoirs which, he said, "should make good 'stuff' for a publication." The memoirs, up to 1927, are in the collection. The person who uses the written material in the collection has to be wary about dates, for Mr. Hurley, while he has a photographic memory for scenes and episodes, has little memory for dates. His memoirs read like a narrative, but the dates for his various jobs follow a pattern which doesn't fit reality. Not that this matters much, but it makes it difficult for any writer about Mr. Hurley's life to adjust his account to facts. The gist of the story, however, is the important thing.

The significant parts of the Hurleyana collection are the scores of slides and the selection of early sketches, the figure drawings he did during the 1930's, and all sorts of designs based on his readings about zoology, entymology, and ichthyology.

The collection is not of much practical use in a library, for the slides and small pictures are not suitable for display, but it could be used as the basis for a splendid hour-long television documentary on Hurley and his work. His career as an artist could be traced on television much more effectively than in any other manner, by showing the artist's sketches, his finished paintings from the sketches (which a good detective could track down), his slides of the landscapes that he made so much his own, and visits to the places where he loved to sketch. The television camera could go into the Legislative Buildings in Regina, the schools, the banks, and some of the homes where his paintings hang; it could go up in the air and photograph the same scenes the flying artist photographed; and it could go into his home for a demonstration of how he created not only his landscapes but also his abstracts. A film about Mr. Hurley would also be a documentary about the face of the Prairies and the changing face of the cities that are burgeoning there, and of the towns that are fading away. The sound effects could make use of Mr. Hurley on his bones in rhythm with some of his favorite music.

The material could be used effectively, too, for an illustrated lecture on the artist, and no doubt as time goes on and his rather unusual place in the history of art in Western Canada becomes clearly evident, it will be so used. The important fact is that a Hurleyana collection has been preserved, a testimony to the foresight of those who organized, accepted, and paid for it and to their belief that the stature of Hurley as an artist is a significant one and yet to be appreciated.

On November the fifteenth, he wrote to Mr. Appelt that he had received the money for the collection. "Believe me," he said, "I got a thrill taking the thousand dollars to deposit into our bank, it being the first in that large amount ever to come into my hands."

The one thousand dollars that Mr. Hurley received for the slides and sketches, diaries and letters might have been the largest amount he had ever received in a lump sum, but news of the sale of one of his paintings by auction for $140 caused even him to wonder if just perhaps he should have put a little higher price on his art. If he had done so, he might have had more than a thousand dollars in the bank to show for a year's work, as he had had, for instance, in 1955—a sum, of course, which represented his savings "even after giving increasingly to the Lord's work." At the time, though, he felt positively rich, for the memory of years on relief still chilled him. The painting which brought what to Hurley was the fantastic sum of $140 was included, he doesn't know how, in a Christie's (Canada) Montreal Book Auction held in Calgary in 1970. In 1972, he still sells his paintings —landscapes and lighthouses—for a sum much less than $140, although he has raised his price from the usual twenty dollars to around forty.

In the late 1960's Mr. Hurley took two new steps. First, he began using acrylic paints (the lighthouse reproduced here is done in acrylics), and although he still uses artists' water colors, he prefers to work with acrylics, as being thicker in consistency, they are easier to handle. With acrylics, for instance, he can use Bristol board with greater assurance that he will achieve the atmospheric effects he wants, but he still prefers pebble board. His creative method is the same with acrylics as with water colors. With a pencil—occasionally with India ink—he sketches in the horizon line and the elevators or whatever structures he intends to include (for straight lines he uses a ruler, for the curved lines in his abstracts he uses a piece of bent cardboard, adding the curved lines on top of the washes or spatterwork by applying paint to the edge of the cardboard), indicates the road, and then starts building up the sky. For blotting out clouds, he uses Kleenex. It's the method he developed from his study of the Richmond-Littlejohns book, and he has found no logical reason to alter it. The use of Kleenex is his adaption for their "loose wad of butter-muslin to produce white clouds."

The second new step, quite a radical one for him, was that he started to write instead of to print, the result of having been given a pen with a special nib as a Christmas gift. With the pen he can produce thick or thin lines at will and he developed a sort of italic script style of writing. Writing takes him less time than printing, and it's easier for his correspondents to decipher.

R. W. Hurley,
445 Walter Avenue,
Victoria, B.C.
(By The Sea)
March 3rd, 1972.

His handwriting

Christmases for the Hurleys in Victoria have become truly joyous occasions, for there are six grandchildren to share them with, three Funks living in Victoria, and three young Hurleys living north of Vancouver where Chuck is employed at the Bridge River Dam. When the young Hurleys come for a visit at 445, the room upstairs—where Isabella stashes her private Hurleyana collection—is turned into a dormitory. The closely knit family group has contributed much to Isabella's and Bob's enjoyment of their life by the sea and has helped to ease them through some of the more difficult times of illness.

In the late fall of 1969 Mr. Hurley was stricken with a heart attack and he was hospitalized for several weeks, during which time he amused himself by watching the pigeons that roosted on his window sill. On release, he had to learn to walk again, and he has been bothered ever since with a skin condition, an allergic reaction, his doctors think, to some of his drugs.

However, most of the children of Charles and Hannah Hurley have been noted, among other things, for their longevity. The oldest, Lizzie, whom Young Bob used to visit in Regent's Park, lived to be eighty-seven. Margaret, two of whose children still live at 28 Oakfield Road; Alice, married to Harry Bull who suggested Canada to Bob; and Charles, the pigeon fancier, soccer player, and pub entertainer, all lived to be ninety. Nellie and Miriam, both well over eighty, are still alive. Arthur, who took Bob to the zoo and to the docks while he did water-color sketches of the activity on the Thames, died from meningitis in 1915. He was buried in Colchester, and Bob and Alice represented the family at the funeral. Robert remembers yet that they heard the ominous sound of cannons from across the Channel, booming the very sound of death, as they stood by the grave.

From the days when he sent drawings to his family to help them to visualize his Canadian life, he has kept in touch. Their names appear intermittently throughout the diaries, a birthday card received, a Christmas present sent. On his sixtieth birthday, 1954, he wrote: "It seems not too long ago that the Hurley sisters were referring to me as Young Bob." And indeed, he was still young in spirit as he added: "I somehow feel I have my best water colors yet to execute."

Since the heart attack, Mr. Hurley hasn't been very mobile. The radio has become his church, and he knows the hours and the stations for the religious programs of his choice on Sundays. The radio, too, is his concert hall, in addition to his record player. There is the hour each morning when he sings hymns and makes contact with the Lord. These he calls his "vitamin sessions." And there are the flowers in the garden, the bird in its cage in the kitchen window, and blank pebble board in his workroom waiting for the touch of his brush. He turned over his stamp collection to Isabella when arthritis forced her into inactivity, and she and Miss Child, who knew the Hurleys from the lab days, spend many evenings at their stamp albums. Bob looks on, but he can't help, for he is blind in one eye and has little vision in the other. The vision he has, he saves for his painting, and he astonishes everyone, including his doctor, with what he is able to accomplish.

Nineteen seventy-one was Homecoming Year in Saskatchewan. The extension division at the University of Saskatchewan in Saskatoon had hoped to include Robert Hurley in some of the observances, and it issued an invitation to him to return. He didn't feel up to making the trip, but Isabella came "home," making happy use of Air Canada's wheel chair service. She had a marvelous time, visiting old friends and catching up on the news. She was very touched to notice, when visiting the homes of young friends who had attended children's parties at Railway Avenue, that they had little framed Hurleys on their walls—postcard-size paintings they had won as prizes in party games. She was also astounded by the change in the appearance of the city and by its growth.

While Isabella was being royally treated in Saskatoon with lunches, teas, dinners, and midnight snacks, Bob probably revived his skill at making pancakes, learned in the lumber camp days, and when he felt the desire for something tastier, he could take the ten-minute walk to the fish and chips shop. And he makes a good cup of tea, which goes well with buttered oat cakes that can be bought at a supermarket.

Hurley returned to Saskatchewan in a sense, however, for his paintings were included in two exhibitions: "Jan Wyers—Robert Hurley, an exhibition of two prairie painters," held in the Norman Mackenzie Art Gallery, Regina, from December the fourth, 1970, to January the third, 1971; and "Watercolour Painters from Saskatchewan," an exhibition organized by the Norman Mackenzie Gallery and circulated by the National Gallery of Canada in 1971-72. It was to have been hung in Victoria in March, and Bob intended to visit the art gallery for the thrill of seeing some of his work in a show again; he doesn't attend art exhibitions because he can't see well enough to enjoy them. Unfortunately, and to his disappointment, there was a mix-up in the exhibition's circuit, and "Watercolour Painters from Saskatchewan" didn't get to Victoria.

In his Introduction to the two-man show, Mr. Fenton, assistant to the director of the Regina gallery, made the following cogent remarks:

"Hurley is a remarkably abstract artist. He has spoken of attempting to paint the prairies in terms of colour washes and simplified design, but apart from admitting to an interest in modern art 'in its saner aspects' and to the influence of John Sell Cotman . . . his sources are difficult to determine. He seems to have developed, virtually on his own, a remarkable sense of colour and proportion and to have discarded, at a time when it was virtually unheard of, any tendency to evoke his sensibility through drawing."

In writing about Mr. Hurley's work in the Introduction to the "Watercolour Painters from Saskatchewan" exhibition, which was of a later date, Mr. Fenton either changed his mind about the influences or he wrote it before he wrote the other introduction, for there he says:

". . . Lindner . . . borrowed the serpentine drawing of *art nouveau*; Robert Hurley seems to have borrowed as well from cubism and Bauhaus design. Two-dimensional design, insofar as it cancels out pictorial space, tends to turn depicted objects into emblems. The single, weathered tree in the foreground of many Group of Seven landscapes is related not only to the drawing and design of *art nouveau,* but also to its use of symbolic motifs . . .

". . . Hurley's relationship to *art nouveau* is less obvious than Lindner's, perhaps because his subjects, derived almost exclusively from the flat prairie, are inherently geometric; but the tapestry-like cloud patterns . . . are reminiscent of *art nouveau,* and the solitary grain elevators that have become his trademark recall the weathered trees of the Group of Seven . . ."

However, to continue with the Introduction to the two-man show, which would have Hurley's approval more than any talk about *art nouveau,* cubism, Bauhaus design, and so forth: ". . . Hurley's drawing is frequently done with a ruler and serves to separate areas of relatively flat colour washes. The pictures tend to be simply divided into land and sky by a horizontal line, with the sky taking up the greater part. . . . Moreover, these poles and buildings do not simply establish recession into the picture, but divide and articulate the colour washes, establishing space and flatness at the same time.

". . . He was not only the first painter in the area to employ flat, colour washes, but seems to have instinctively realized that these colour areas had to be judiciously proportioned. Hurley is one of the rare, contemporary landscape painters who appears to be concerned with the shape of his pictures, who realizes that the shape and size of the picture rectangle alters the shape and size of the areas within it and alters, in turn, the various divisions which occur within those areas. He has also anticipated colour painting by his sheer ability as a colourist; he knows, as few artists do, how to use subtle variations of value and hue to evoke, rather than simply depict, light and atmosphere.

"Painting the prairies is difficult because . . . there is no place to employ drawing to establish volumes and space. One need only examine the work of Lawren Harris, the other great simplifier in Canadian landscape painting, to see what a distinct bearing this fact has upon the nature of their respective pictures. . . . Hurley's pictures frequently appear to be luminous totalities. This is particularly evident in the wonderful series of night and evening pictures which he produced during the forties and fifties, pictures which produce the impression of darkness without being, in themselves, dark, pictures which achieve their luminosity through colour relationship rather than through graphic or plastic means.

"Despite his virtues, Hurley remains a modest, provincial painter. He has never abstracted his work successfully beyond the immediate substance of his vision, which remains the Saskatchewan prairies. He has seldom painted the lakes, rivers and valleys of Saskatchewan with success. His rather stylized abstractions of birds, fish, etc. of the late 1950s were uniformly disappointing. Since moving to Victoria . . . his continuing inspiration seems to stem from the prairies. Two recent pictures, done no doubt from colour notes or slides, are as daring and central to his vision as anything he has done."

Mr. Fenton's summing up of Hurley's virtues and weaknesses as an artist is the most comprehensive and critical to have appeared to date. He has certainly spelled out for those who treasure their Hurley skies, particularly the nocturnes, the reasons for the tremendous appeal of the paintings—their "luminous totality." Mr. Hurley himself did not consider his sunrises, sunsets, and nocturnes to be so creative as some of his other landscapes and as his abstracts. The great demand for his sky studies forced him to paint them almost to order. He always knew when they were successful and when they weren't, but he didn't take the same joy in their creation as he did when he felt that he had captured the distance and space of the Prairies or when he built up an abstract that expressed his strong sense of the rhythm and harmony of all nature, which he valued most of all as he considered them to be the most "creative."

"End of Yorath Island," done with dry brush technique, is one landscape he likes because of its "feeling" and his success with the cirrus clouds (Plate XVI); "Champagne Fantasy," so named by Mr. Wickenden when he first laid eyes on it, is one of his more "musical" abstracts, with its circular motif and its compositional use of colors, and it is one which he still likes. (Plate XX)

To the charge that he remains "a modest, provincial artist," most would agree with the "modest," many would question the "provincial," in the sense of being "narrow" or "limited." He is a modest artist because he is a modest man. Essentially a lyricist, it would have been quite out of character for Hurley to have tried to express himself in grand or epic terms. To describe his art as "modest" is to define its style, not its quality, for in some of his paintings he came as close to perfection in achieving what he was attempting as is given to any artist. He was ambitious only in his striving after a modest perfection and in the energy he spent painting hundreds upon hundreds of his "colored drawings." As for being "provincial," Hurley's vision was not so much limited by his environment as it was set free. The Prairies offered him, as few environments could, the fundamental principles of nature, as set down by Richmond and Littlejohns—"unity, simplicity, vitality, and repose." The man, the time, the place, were perfectly matched. As Hurley would say, with his religious approach to happenings, the circumstance of his being on the Canadian plains in the twentieth century was not fortuitous but a Divine Plan.

He wrote to *The Prophetic Expositor,* the monthly publication of the British-Israel World Federation, in 1971:

"Dear Mrs. Cunningham—To celebrate my 77th birthday, I am enclosing a cheque in support of the ministry. I owe all I have to our God, the Lord and Saviour. I feel like making this a very special letter. Am enclosing a recent catalogue of an Art Exhibit of some of my paintings held in Regina. . . .

"You and Mr. Halliwell, I am sure, will enjoy looking through this catalogue. The fact that I had only a grade 6, London, English primary education, makes the art success all the more a testimony to what God can do to a 'Sinner saved by Grace.' "

The brief letter contains three facts that are very prominent in Mr. Hurley's story. First, the sending of a check "in support of the ministry." Since he first earned any money beyond what he needed for his simple wants, he has contributed to a variety of ministries. Secondly, he has never managed to conquer the sense of insecurity, almost inferiority, deriving from his grade six education. It rears its head again in his most recent letter when answering a query about the number of paintings owned by the Vice-Regal party of Governor General Vanier: "This is a fantastic true story. As I only had a meagre London Council Schooling up to Grade 6." Thirdly, regarding art success as a testimony to what God can do, Mr. Hurley has never doubted that it was God's plan for him to paint the Prairies with the God-given talent the Prairies had helped to reveal.

When Dr. Anstensen was presenting the case for the establishment of the Hurleyana collection at the University of Saskatchewan, he wrote to the head of one department: "In my opinion Robert Hurley will be remembered as a significant Canadian artist."

According to Mr. Fenton, in the late 1930's Hurley "became the first genuine painter of the prairies." If the Prairies are accepted in the Canadian nation as more than a place which produces superb wheat, then there is no doubt that Mr. Hurley should be regarded as a significant Canadian artist. Even at the present time his paintings have gathered enough critical acclaim, not to mention popular worship, to justify their representation in the Canadiana section of the National Gallery. His province of Saskatchewan and the university in his province have done proudly by him, and they would be quite willing to share him with people in the rest of the country.

In the meantime, what Dan Worden said when he closed his 1955 interview serves well to write "thirty" to Hurley's biography—"This has been Robert Newton Hurley—the Saskatchewan painter who sees God in a sunset."

Plates

Credit Box

We wish to thank the many persons who made their private collections of Hurley paintings available to us. There are those whose paintings appear in this volume, there are others whose paintings we viewed but which for reasons of similarity we were unable to include when the final selection of plates was made. To all we are greatly indebted.

Owners: Dr. and Mrs. A. Anstensen—XXVII
Dr. and Mrs. Harold R. Baker—VI
Dr. and Mrs. E. W. Barootes—III, XXVI
Mrs. A. L. Caldwell—XXV
Mr. and Mrs. A. J. E. Child—II, XV, XXIX
Mrs. F. M. Froom—XII
Mr. and Mrs. Alvin Funk—XVII, XVIII
Mr. and Mrs. R. J. Graham—XXX, XXXII
Jim and Grace Hogg—V
Dr. R. P. Knowles—p.76
Mrs. R. Knowles—p. 86
Dr. and Mrs. Lorne Paul—IV
Mr. and Mrs. W. Perehudoff—XI, p. 32 and 38
Mrs. R. C. Russell—VII, IX, XXI, XXIII
Saskatoon Public Library—X
Dr. and Mrs. Norman Ward—XXIV·
Mr. and Mrs. H. W. Wickenden—XXII

The originals of some paintings were not available and use had to be made of 35mm. slides produced many years ago; reproduction of these has been done in reduced size to minimize defects in quality of the slides.

In many cases the artist did not date his paintings, and the dates assigned in this book represent approximations only.

Nocturne

1971. 15 x 12''

II

R.A.M.HURLEY. 1953

1953. 12 x 10"

Sunset

III

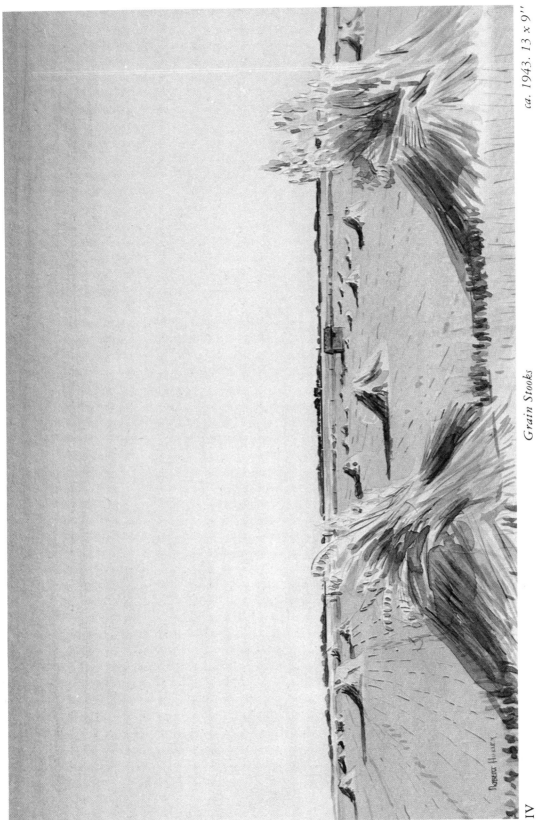

IV

Grain Stooks ca. 1943. 13 x 9''

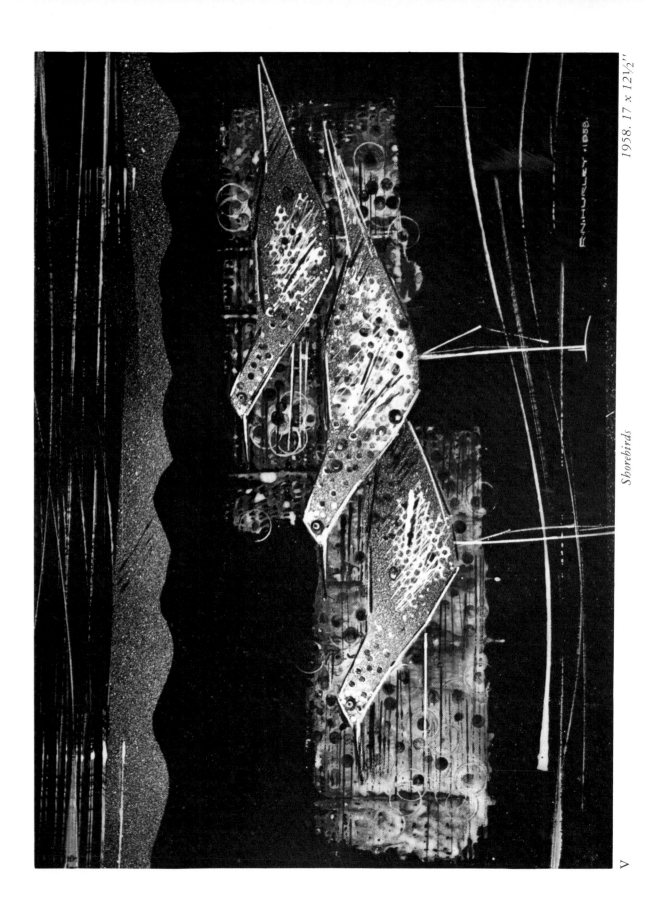

Shorebirds 1958. 17 x 12½"

V

R.N.HURLEY

City at Night   *ca. 1960. 14 x 11"*

VII

Lumber Camp

1943. 13 x 8½''

VIII   Quibell, Ontario   1926. 6½ x 4½'', actual size.

IX   *Cottonwood, Goldeye Bay*   *1936. 8½ x 12″*

Tipperary Creek

ca. 1938. 14 x 12''

X

XI   *Still Life*   *1944. 5½ x 7'' actual size.*

Ⅲ 👁 SUPPOSE THE MENDEL ART COST 100,000 DOLLARS OR MAYBE DOUBLE THAT BUT IN MY OPINION MOST OF IT IS "WACKY" COMPUTER. MUCH OF THAT "MODERN" JUNK I WOULD NOT GIVE IT SPACE IN OUR GARAGE. HOWEVER A TERRIFIC SOBERED UP THE COMPANY AT 10.30 P.M.

OUR CHARLES. ELAINE. LENNIE UP FROM CITY FOR SUNDAY.

T.M. WEDNESDAY 👁 BOARD A FOR THE WELL MANY THIN. YEARS OLD TIME, TWO MORE DAYS AND MY BATCHIN' DAYS WILL BE ENDED MAKING FIVE WEEKS ON MY OWN. SO UNTIL OUR VICTORIA SAFARI IS OVER 👁 WILL SAY SO LONG

(DID YOU SEE MY T.V. DEBUT? C.K.C.K.)

ROBERT NATHANIEL HURLEY.

(BEST REGARDS TO YOUR DAD.)

XIII   *Quaker Oats Mill   1948. 14 x 10''*

XIV   *The Storm Cloud   1959. 18 x 11''*

XV *Queen Elizabeth Power Plant 1960. 14½ x 11''*

XVI   *End of Yorath Island   1950. 14 x 10''*

XVII *The Crystals* *1953. 20 x 12"*

XVIII *Herons 1953. 14 x 17½"*

XIX *Guitar Mozartian* *1953. 18 x 11"*

XX *Champagne Fantasy* *1956. 20 x 12"*

Sutherland

ca. 1949. 12 x 10"

XXII   *Reflections*   *ca. 1947. 11½ x 8½"*

1952. 13½ x 9½"

Barnes Lake

XXIII

XXIV   G.T.P. Bridge, Autumn   1953. 10½ x 8½"

XXV

Spring Thaw

1958. 14½ x 10″

XXVI   *Northern Saskatchewan Lake*   *1959. 17 x 12½"*

Aerial Landscape

XXVII

Fisgard Lightbouse

1972. 15½ x 12"

XXVIII

Sky at Dawn

XXIX

Sky, Winter Day

1961. 14 x 10''

XXX

XXXI   *Winter Scene*   *undated, 14 x 18″*

XXXII   *Sunset*   *1961. 14 x 10″*

INDEX